I0677556

ORPHEU
LITERARY QUARTERLY VOLUMES 1 & 2

ORPHEU

LITERARY QUARTERLY

VOL. 1 & 2

TRANSLATED FROM PORTUGUESE BY
David Swartz

WITH A PREFACE BY
Nuno Júdice

COPYRIGHT © 2021 by David Swartz
COVER DESIGN by David Swartz
BACK COVER ART by David Swartz, *Reintegration of Hand & Eye* (2007)
INTERIOR DESIGN by Alexandru Oprescu

All rights reserved. Published by New Meridian, part of the non-profit organization New Meridian Arts, 2021.

No part of this publication may be reproduced, or stored in a retrieval system, or transmitted in any form or by any means, electronic, mechanical, photocopying, or otherwise, without written permission of the publisher, except in the case of brief quotations in reviews. For information regarding permission, write to newmeridianarts1@gmail.com

LIBRARY OF CONGRESS CATALOGING-IN-PUBLICATION DATA

Orpheu — Literary Quarterly — Vol. 1 & 2
Authored by David Swartz

ISBN: 9781737249160
LCCN: 2022930166

This translation would not have been made possible without the generous support of Direção-Geral do Livro, dos Arquivos e das Bibliotecas and Camões, IP. We are sincerely grateful.

The Magazine
that made
a Generation

ORPHEU — *REVISTA TRIMESTRAL DE LITERATURA* was published in 1915. The project was to be a quarterly magazine, the first issue corresponding to the months of January to March and the second from April to June. A third, of which proofs remain, was never completed or launched due to lack of money to print it. The title is the result of a commitment to the symbolist tendency of Luís de Montalvor, who wrote the introduction, and of the fact that among the collaborators there was a Brazilian poet, Ronald de Carvalho, who wanted the magazine to reach the public in Brazil. A title suggested for the magazine by Mário de Sá-Carneiro, *Europa*, was put aside to make room for this reference to the classical myth of Orpheus, which contradicts the cosmopolitan and futuristic side of Sá-Carneiro's poems, the "Maritime Ode" of Álvaro de Campos, and the paintings of Santa-Rita Pintor. In July 1914, Sá-Carneiro wrote in a letter to Pessoa "A *Europa*! A *Europa*! como ela seria necessária!..."[1] However, the desire to reach a Portuguese-speaking public, at a time when everything that came from Portugal echoed beyond the Atlantic, was stronger.

With its variety of contributors, from symbolists to futurists, *Orpheu* was an eclectic magazine, opening space to all the trends of Portuguese Modernism. Among those trends were: Paulismo, the expression of a late form of decadent Symbolism; Intersectionism, created by Fernando Pessoa in his poem "Oblique Rain" to designate a poetry that results from multiple lines and planes of images and meanings, like that of Cubism in the plastic arts; and Futurism, either in the form of the reproductions of works by Santa-Rita Pintor (Guilherme de Santa-Rita, 1889-1918), or in the form of

[1] *"Europa! Europa!* this is what our age requires!..."

poems by Álvaro de Campos, the heteronym of Fernando Pessoa, whose work comes closest to this aesthetic, despite later preferring to call himself a Sensationist. The collection also contained Mário de Sá-Carneiro's "Poems without support" which follow, perhaps with a touch of parody, the technical principles of Marinetti's Manifesto, and the collaboration of José de Almada-Negreiros (1893-1970) whose prose poems, while not belonging entirely to Futurism, prefigure a new poem that would come out in a third issue, which ended up not being published. The poem was called "A Cena do Ódio" or "The Scene of Hate". In this poem, both provocative in tone and form, violence takes on the mood of futurist poetry. It was recited by the poet at a coffee table at the café "A Brasileira" in Lisbon's Chiado, in what must have been the first futuristic performance in Portugal, later followed by a rally in 1917 at the Teatro República (now S. Luís) in Lisbon.

The magazine *Orpheu* was attacked by journalistic critics and personalities of the cultural life of the time as being the work of lunatics, worthy of being interned in a madhouse, as was the case of the poet Ângelo de Lima whose poems were produced in psychotic delirium while interned in Rilhafoles, a Lisbon-based prison hospital for the insane. Contrary to what was intended, this scandal contributed to the enormous visibility of this new generation whose importance was acknowledged by relevant magazines such as "Ilustração portuguesa"[2] which published their photographs and called them avant-garde innovators, with Paris as their epicenter. The arrival of Futurism in Portugal in 1915 spoke to the mental and cultural transformations taking place during this time, to which these two volumes bear witness.

Independently of the evolution that each of the magazine's collaborators would undergo after 1915, the generation of *Orpheu*, with all its diversity of expressions, from the most conservative to the most radical, represents one of the most profound revolutions in the language and themes of Portuguese literature, with traces that extended into the 20th century and which remain both alive and unmatched up until this day.

NUNO JÚDICE

---

[2] "Portuguese Illustration"

> *Sinto na minha mão, não sei como, a chave de uma porta desconhecida.*
> I know not how, but I feel in my hand, the key to an unknown door.
> — THE SEAFARER, *FERNANDO PESSOA*

My translation of *Orpheu* is, for me, the key to an unknown door. My initial motive was simply to read it; to do so, I needed to translate it. I am grateful for having the opportunity to share my reading with the public and for the different kinds of support I've received while translating it. I think it is a volume of Beauty and welcomes an international audience. Notwithstanding, the exquisite rhymes and onomatopoeic reality of these poems will be completely lost on English readers. The consolation I offer is the attempt to capture their spirit as a whole, to the best of my ability.

Collectively, the poems in *Orpheu 1 & 2* reveal a turn inwards towards a way of looking at oneself as the other, encapsulating the absent-present, feminine-masculine, nowhere-everywhere union at the core of art and life. This unique and utterly enchanted poetic vision initiates an interior adventure in which, with the poet's dreaming hands at the helm, "silence begins to take shape, begins to be something" (*The Seafarer*, Fernando Pessoa):

> *No alvor das minhas mãos chora a distância*
> *proas rachadas, longes de ouro, ideais...*

> In the dawn of my hands the distance cries
> Cracked prows, remoteness of gold, ideals...
> — THE PASSING SOUL, *RONALD DE CARVALHO*

Silence, like nothing, simply doesn't exist! As a result, our invocation to nothing, to silence, can only give birth to more of what does not exist, and hence, to what is not subject to the passage of time:

Auréola de Dor, que finaliza
Na noite do abismo do meu nada;
Silêncio, prece, comunhão sagrada,
Sombra de luz que em Ti me diviniza,

Halo of Sorrow that ends
In the night of the abyss of my nothingness,
Silence, prayer, holy communion,
Dream of light that divinizes myself in You,

— AGONY, CÔRTES-RODRIGUES

Our poet's "holy communion," with silence and nothing originates a "Dream of light that divinizes" the ever present future reader, to whom these words, in my view, are ultimately addressed.

MY TRANSLATION OWES A GREAT DEAL to the editorial assistance of Mónica Sofia Gomes Ganhão, who over the past year has provided me with copious notes and suggestions in addition to meeting with me regularly to go over the text in Portuguese and English. My gratitude to her is immense. Her assistance, contribution and support for this project cannot be overstated.

As *Orpheu's* release in English drew near, I met with three Portuguese English students at the New University of Lisbon: Rui da Cunha Viana Guerra, Megan Enza Martucci, and Adriana Albuquerque Colaço, all remarkable for their poetic talents and editorial expertise, who over a period of 10 days, in shifts and altogether as a group, read over my translation with me from start to finish (with an eye on the original Portuguese). They isolated punctuation inconsistencies, variances in meaning, and provided useful suggestions. Their contribution to this translation was vital.

The appreciation, confidence and support I've received for this project from Nava Renek, Alexandra Carides, and Alexandru Oprescu has made all the difference.

Finally, I'd like to thank my wife Carla whose rich spirit and love have been fuel to my fire.

DAVID SWARTZ
Lisboa, Portugal,
November 2021

"ORPHEU"

LITERARY QUARTERLY

PORTUGAL AND BRAZIL

Copyright: ORPHEU Ltd   Editor: ANTONIO FERRO

DIRECTORS

PORTUGAL

Luiz de Montalvôr — 17, Caminho do Forno do Tijolo — LISBON

BRAZIL

Ronald de Carvalho — 104, Rua Humaytá — RIO DE JANEIRO

YEAR I — 1915   N.º 1   January-February-March

CONTENTS

Cover Page Designed by José Pacheco

Offices: Tipografia do Comércio — 10, Rua da Oliveira, at Carmo

LISBON

CONDITIONS

———

All mail ought to be addressed to the Directors.

We invite only Artists whose sympathy is with the nature of this Journal to collaborate with us. The original texts that are not included will be returned.

Our trustees in Portugal are Srs. Monteiro & C.ª, Livraria Brazileira — 190 and 192, Rua Aurea, Lisbon.

Orpheu will publish an uncertain number of pages, never less than 72, at the invariable price of 30 cents per issue, in Portugal, and 1$500 reis in Brazil.

———

SUBSCRIPTIONS

(PER YEAR — SERIES OF 4 ISSUES)

Portugal, Spain and Portuguese Colonies	1 escudo
Brazil.	5 $ 000 réis **(weak currency)**
Postal Union.	6 francs

Livraria Brazileira de MONTEIRO & C.ia — Publishers

190 and 192, RUA AUREA — LISBON

For sale at the end of April:

SKY ON FIRE

NOVELLAS BY

MARIO DE SÁ-CARNEIRO

GREAT SHADOW — MYSTERY
MAN OF DREAMS — WINGS — I-MYSELF THE OTHER
THE STRANGE DEATH OF PROF. ANTENA
THE FIXER OF INSTANTS — RESURRECTION

1 VOLUME OF 350 PAGES

COVER DESIGN BY

JOSÉ PACHECO

Price 70 cents

Works by collaborators of this volume

Luiz de Montalvôr
On the Way, a booklet of verses . . . .
Published by Livraria Brazileira
Price: 20 cents

Mario de Sá-Carneiro
Friendship, a play in 3 acts (in collaboration with Tomás Cabreira J.^{or})
Published by Livraria Bordalo
Price: 30 cents

Beginning, novellas. . . . .
Published by Livraria Ferreira
Price: 70 cents

Dispersion, 12 poems . . . .
Published by the author
Sold Out

The Confessions of Lucio, a narrative. . .
Published by the author
Price: 60 cents

Ronald de Carvalho
Glorious Light, poems. . . . .
Paris 1913. Published by the author

Fernando Pessoa
The seven rooms of the abandoned palace, poems. . . . .
In preparation

Alfredo Pedro Guisado
Rimes of Night and Sadness, verses. . .
Published by Livraria Classica Editora
Price: 40 cents

Distance, poems . . . .
Published by Livraria Ferreira
Price: 30 cents

José de Almada-Negreiros
Frizos, prose illustrated by the author. .
To be released this year

Alvaro de Campos
Arch of Triumph . . . .
In preparation

Some of these works may be directly requested from the administration of ORPHEU — Alfredo Pedro Guisado: 112, Rocio, Lisboa.

In our second issue (coming out in June) we intend to publish, among other works, the following: *Poems* by Fernando Pessoa, *Interior World*, a novella by Mario de Sá-Carneiro and *Narcissus*, a poem by Luiz de Montalvôr.

The cover illustration was created in the studios of the ILLUSTRATORS

ORPHEU

Vol. I — 1915

ORPHEU

———

LITERARY QUARTERLY

———

VOLUME I

LISBON

Typographia do Commercio

10, Rua da Oliveira (at Carmo), 10

1915

INTRODUCTION

———

With respect to its title and purpose ORPHEU *refuses to be a conventional journal, affirming the right to create art by disassociating itself from uncharacteristic or fragmentary styles: a remarkable feat for our volume of Beauty, given the literary precedence of making magazines and journals in these ways.*

Our intentions are pure and rare, as is our destiny of Exile in Beauty!

Properly speaking, ORPHEU *is an exile of artistic temperaments seeking art as secrecy or torment…*

Our ambition is to materialize, as a group or idea, a determined number of revelations in thought or art, that, based on this aristocratic principle, find in ORPHEU, *their esoteric ideal, ingrained in the way we feel and know ourselves.*

The portrait of a generation, race or milieu, often called literature, with its immediate world on exhibition, is the sum of what other journals attempt to achieve with their variety, annulling any attempt at art by maintaining the sameness of their subjects (articles, sections or moments). — None of this matters in the case of ORPHEU.

This explains our anxiety and our essence!

In line with this approach to Beauty, ORPHEU *seeks life and palpitation. It is not fair for those who dream these thoughts proudly in lavish splendor to sterilize themselves individually and in isolation — on the contrary, they should join in and share with others who are of the same rare and interior nature, waiting anxiously*

*and dreaming of something they lack, resulting in an aesthetics of permutations
between the ones who look for us and the ones we wait for...*

Those involved in the structure and formation of ORPHEU, *will compete
within the same level of competence for the same elevated, united and discreet
rhythm, upon which the aesthetic harmony of its specialty depends.*

*And thus we'd like to follow some of these desires for good taste and refined
purposes in art, that currently live in isolation, certain that as pioneers of our
time, we shall reveal a sign of life, something praiseworthy, expecting effort, con-
tentment and consideration from those who form the public readership, towards
the realization of the literary work of* ORPHEU.

LUÍS DE MONTALVÔR.

FROM "HINTS OF GOLD"

POEMS BY

MARIO DE SÁ-CARNEIRO

Taciturn

There is Gold inlaid inside me with rare stones
Profound joy of my Soul, precious lights —
Sinister Gold in sounds of medieval bronze
Triangular ciborium of infernal rites.

In my inner world armors closed,
Iron helmets crush Princesses.
A whole royal strain of heroes of Other braveries
Are stripped of their shields and prey inside me.

Heraldic moonlight over throes of ruby,
Humiliations in lily, brocade vengeance;
Bazilicas of boredom, harnesses of wrinkles
Insignias of Illusion, trophies of jasper and October…

The dull drawbridge of I-have-been
Rusted — in vain they will attempt to close it…
Over Vacant moats, battlements of still-wanting —
Mornings of arms remain in camps of oblivion…

I walk through myself in halls without windows or doors,
Long throne rooms in thick densities,
Where pans of Tapestries are nostalgically frayed
And the divans, all around, forgetfully absorb my cravings…

Purple ends of Empire resign inside me —
Satin whims of my Astral disdain…
Funeral rites of heroes in my feudal pain —
And my remorse are terraces over the Sea…

Paris — August 1914

SALOMÉ

Purple Insomnia. Light punctuating in fear,
Dead light of the moon, more Soul than moon...
She dances, she grinds. Her flesh, alcohol of naked
Spreads out for me in a spasm of secrecy...

Everything is whimsical around her, in fatuous shadows...
Her shattered, maddening aroma, caprioled in color...
I am cold... Alabaster!... My Soul stopped...
And her body glides into projecting statues...

She calls me in Iris. She halos herself to lose me,
She gushes her naked breasts towards me, echoes my weakness...
Seals, helmets, daggers... The madwoman wants to end me:

Biting herself crying — there are sexes in her weeping...
I rise in sound, oscillate and depart, I go, I burn myself
In the imperial mouth that humanized a Saint...

Lisbon 1913 – November 3

A CERTAIN REDDISH VOICE IN THE NIGHT...

An elusive sortilege this voice, opiated
In amaranthine sounds, nights of uncertainty,
That I remember I know not from Where — the voice of a
Princess Dancing half-naked between flashes of swords.

Leonine, she hurls the purplish meat;
Self-intoxicated, panting with Beauty,
Sharpens her naked breasts, uncovers her sex...
Prays with spasmic struggle in copulating Soul...

Though I never saw her, even in a vision. Only
Her voice centers her in my remembrance. But I
I do not desire her flesh — the non-existent flesh...

She is only made of voice-in-heat, the astral ballerina —
And in this voice — Statue, ah! in this total-voice,
I dream of vanishing into vices of ivory...

Lisbon 1914 — January 31

OUR LADY OF PARIS

Dashes of sound advance towards me flogging me
In light.
Vibrating all over, I flee... Where will I find shelter?...
The arms of a cross
Yearn inside me and I flee the moonlight too...

The smell of the sea
Refreshes me,
Distant melody
Longing for the Sea...
Myrtles and tamarinds
Scent the distance;
Beautiful dreams slide...
But Gold does not endure,
And now the night grows into collapsing cathedrals...
I lay buried under wax candles —
I darken myself in delirium,
But I too resurrect from Ideals...

— My senses draining themselves...
Altars and candles...
Pride... Stars...
Stained glass! Stained glass!

Fleur-de-lis...

Blots of color spring warheads...
Great ships consecrating themselves...
— Our Lady of Paris!...

Paris 1913 — June 15

This inconstancy of myself in vibration
Shall transpose me into intermediate zones,
Where I'll follow between crystals of disquietude
Clinking, undulating... Reins released,
My dreams, lions of fire and awe tamed to guide
The tower of gold that was the car of my Soul,
Wander through the desert, moribund from Moonlight.
I will only remember myself in the swaying of a palm-tree...
In the oasis, afterwards, edges abyss themselves,
The atmosphere may be different, on other planes:
Where frogs would croak at me in hoarse human tones
Vomiting my flesh that they had eaten with manure...

*

There is always a great Arch at the bottom of my eyes...
At each step my soul is another cross,
And my heart gyrates: it is a wheel of colors...
I do not know where I am going, nor do I see what I pursue...
I no longer follow the trace of my trace of gold...
I slip on bridges of jelly and mold...
Today, the light for me is always a half-light...

. . . .
. . . .

The tables of the Cafe went mad like air...
Now one of my arms falls... Look, how it goes waltzing about
In a tailcoat, through the halls of the Viceroy...

(I climb myself up like a staircase of rope,
And my Unnerving Pain is a broken trapeze...).

Lisbon — May 1914

DISTANT MELODY

In a dream of Iris, murdered in gold and ember,
Memories come to me of another blue Time
Oscillating between veils of tule —
A slender and light time, — a Winged time.

Then, my senses were colors,
My longings were born in a garden,
In my soul there were Other distances —
The journey of following those Distances was flowers...

Gold fell if I mused Stars,
Moonlight beat down over my self-estrangement...
Night-lagoons, how beautiful you were
Under terraces-de-lis of self-memory!

Age-chord from Between dream and Moon,
Where fleeting hours are always jade,
Where mist was a longing,
And the light — the yearnings of a naked Princess...

Bannisters of sound, arches of Loving,
Bridges of brightness, perfumed spires...
Unspeakable Dominion of Opium and fire
That I will never again inhabit in color...

Carpets of other Persias more Orient...
Curtains of China more ivory...
Auroreal Temples of satin rites...
Fountains flowing shade, gently...

Pinnacle-pantheons of nostalgias...
Cathedrals of being-Me over the sea...
Staircases of honor, staircases alone, in the open air...
New Byzantian-souls, other Turkeys...

Fluid memories... ash of brocade...
Waves of unreal indigos inside me...
— In my circle, I am an exiled King,
Vagabond of a mermaid's dream...

Paris 1914 — June 30

GLIMPSE

Frail, autumnal hours —
Through sorrowful day's ends —
My Soul is cold water
In amphoras of Gold… between crystals…

Camarate — Quinta da Vitória.
October 1914

SUGGESTION

The lovers I didn't have,
I feel them crying for me, veiled,
At sunset, about the gardens…
My pain of dead hands
Over satin revives
In their blue sorrow…

Paris — August 1914

<u>7</u>

I am not I nor am I the other,
I am something in between:
      Pillar of the bridge of tedium
      That goes from me to the Other.

Lisbon — February 1914

ANGLE

Where shall I go in this lost immensity,
In this hollow sea of dead certainties?
In the end, all the doors that I thought
I had built in the dike are fakes,

Barges of my tiger-patterned impulses,
— Which ocean has numbed you in Secret?
What wrecked you, enchanted cargos,
What rock did you collide with in a soul of purple?...

— Oh festive ship, oh auburn adventure
Where my longing sailed in Champagne,
Have you also broken apart or, perhaps,
Anchored in Gold in ports of alchemy?...

. . . .
. . . .

Galleons arrived at the bay
With seven Princesses who died.
Regattas of moonlight did not run...
Flags veiled themselves in prayers...

I stopped at the bridge and leaned over,
But the bridge was fake — and about to collapse
I continued along the pier. The pier cambered,
False pier without the sea at its edge...

— Above what I am not there are great bridges
That an other wants to cross only half way
In mirages of false horizons —
An other that I cannot enchain...

Barcelona — September 1914

The Unequaled

Oh, how I wanted you dressed in violets
And frail satin…
Your long ivory finger
Shadowed by black jewels…

And so feverish and delicate
That you could not take a step —
Dreaming stars, distraught,
With prints of color in your lap…

I wanted you naked and cold
Snuggling yourself in —
Sleepy sables,
Auburn ethers and morphines…

Oh! that your nostalgias were silver rattles —
Your frenzies, spangles;
And the idleness in which you falter
Dissipating Moonlight…

. . . .
. . . .

I wanted your kisses of tule
Transparently crimson —
Your spasms of silk…

— Cold clear water on a blue night,
Your love for me should be like Water…

Lisbon 1915 — February 16

APOTHEOSIS

Broken masts, I sail into a sea of Gold
Sleeping fire, uncertain, distant...
Everything was leveled for me in a shallow dream
And today I live in only half of myself...

What I still cry for are bronze sorrows —
Dead pilasters, marbles in the Sunset...
My yearnings were layered with white slabs
And false cloisters where I never prayed...

I came down from myself. I folded the astral mantle,
I broke the cup made of crystal and bewilderment,
I carved into shadow the Gold of my trace...

I ended... Hours-platinum... Aroma-brocade...
Moonlight-yearning... Light-lost... Orchids weeping...

. . . .

— Oh swamps of Myself — stagnant garden...

Paris 1914 — June 28

MARIO DE SÁ-CARNEIRO.

POEMS

BY

RONALD DE CARVALHO

The passing soul

I — Sense

I flee from myself the way an old perfume
undulating and vague, escapes from a missal
and imagine a strange soul walking with me in tune,
saying goodbye to an unreal adventure.

I am transparency, pale flame, yearning,
the last ship to abandon the pier.
In the dawn of my hands the distance cries
Cracked prows, remoteness of gold, ideals…

I dream of my body as of an absentee,
I wake up in a convalescent garden,
I am shipwrecked and exiled inside memory,

I wander in this garden lost in others,
and feel in the flash of final glory
the shadow of what I am dying inside me…

II — Legend

Life is a grief-stricken princess
in her castle of rubies and opals,
playing on a silent harp in the sunset
an agony of souls and speech…

I gather the sad rose from your hands,
The shadow of your life crumbles over me.
You pass, and in your nostalgically rippling shade
Phantoms wander through deserted rooms…

(Lost voices, haphazard oaths,
footsteps that die upon footsteps, bells
wake the dawns inside of me.

And between horns, drums and shrapnel,
clefs, organs, tubas and violins,
Life and Pain begin the battle…)

III — Genesis

Before my soul had been lost,
it was a stone rolling along a path
topaz, opal, forgotten pearl
in a royal bracelet; it was stalk and thorn,

bronze to the touch, golden remnant
lying among the ruins of a barren country,
and the eye of Life reflected, fatally,
in the bloody body of a strange wine...

It was medieval spear and shield,
it was lunar light and wandering lantern,
and after rising, sad, from everything

it came to weep in my being
the bitter curse of being eternal
the pain of being reborn when I die...

NOCTURNAL LIGHT

Dizzy from sleep and sweetness
at the peak of ivory claws
lost in shadow searching light.
Someone died inside me...

A perfume of bitterness rises
through the sad and darkened window
that opens to balconies over the garden
Someone died inside me...

With your fine luxurious
dagger you silently sever
the last rose in the final vase...

And now the naked stem reflects
in your eyes like a fountain
that implores blueness and does not delay...

Unknown tower

From the shadow it rises and does not delay
in the hands that eagerly gird it
the air has always fascinated it
and it washes the luminous lines

The shape troubles the outside light
dreaming painful chimeras
and in the stem of the hour does not bloom
not even the voluptuousness of other roses

Just from being unique it raises
the stone like a smile
that cherishes the sound of bronzes

From the shadow it rises to glory
and the hand that deflowers it is cold clay
in a white flight of memory

In Praise of Fountains

Pain of the fountains agonizing in the Sunset
in feathers and ivories, in roses of gold and light…
Song of the water that descends in dust, light and gentle,
song of the water that rises where the garden is translucent.

Bells sleep in the haze — caressing ashes…
Shadows of ancient ships, tall sails blowing,
cross the very bottom of the swirling lakes,
(the adventure, the conquest, the eternal longing for the sea!)

Fountains dying over themselves, slowly —
curved fans opening and closing in a huff,
a vanquished hand that comes from vain inducements…
— nervous hand, even fuller of desire…

Voluptuous refuge — to be far away, to be distant,
and to return right back to the pier and to leave again!
Voluptuousness — to desire but not possess, to be yearning…
Fountains descending, fountains ascending…

Unfixed emotions, the voluptuousness of forgetting them,
walking within oneself lost in memory…
(Ideal hunters of worlds and stars —
fountains in the Sunset filled with woe and glory…)

The pain of fountains singing in the sunset!
despair, joy — the lip, the hand… and a kiss.
The pain of the fountains, bleeding pain, dreaming pain…
to touch the illusion and die in desire…

REFLEXES
(Poem of the infirm Soul)

My soul trembles like a lily
inside the water of your eyes —
my soul trembles like a lily,
with its hands lashed by thistles.

All draped in the linen of betrothal,
trembling at your door,
all draped in the linen of betrothal
my soul will dawn.

There is a scent of beyond-death
in its aching voice,
there is a scent of beyond-death
in the pale robes of life…

The lilac hour unfolds
in flowers of ash and ember,
the lilac hour unfolds with
a somnambulant winged murmur.

The ships pray through the channel
full of grace and glory…
the ships pray through the channel
the sad history of memory…

My soul awakens the desert pier
blooming in roses of sorrow —
my soul awakens the desert pier
and its shadow is a swan in the water…

And over extinct lamps
fall funerary antennas,
and over extinct lamps
the last moths die.

The towers brood through space.
In the silence violins wander —
the towers brood through space…
in the gloom bells think…

My whole soul encloses itself
in the garden that turned into twilight…
my whole soul encloses itself
in an unreal kiss that was not born…

Inside the water of your eyes
my soul shakes like a lily…

RONALD DE CARVALHO

THE SEAFARER

———

A STATIC DRAMA IN ONE SCENE

to Carlos Franco.

A room which is undoubtably in an old castle. From inside the room you can see that it's circular. To the center, on a bier, is a damsel in white lying in a coffin. Four torches at the corners. To the right, almost in front of those imagining the room, there is a single window, high and narrow, where only a small space of sea can be seen, between two distant hills.

Three damsels watch over the corpse by the window. The first is seated in front of the window, with her back against the torch to the top right. The other two are seated on either side of the window.

It is night and there is a vague remnant of moonlight.

First watcher. — Yet there is nothing to tell us the time.

Second. — We wouldn't be able to hear it. There is no clock here. In a little while it will be morning.

Third. — No: the horizon is black.

First. — Don't you wish, my sister, for us to entertain ourselves by telling each other what we've been? It's beautiful and always false…

Second. — No, let's not speak of that. Besides, have we ever really been anything?

First. — Perhaps. I don't know. But still, it is always beautiful to speak of the past… The hours have passed and we've been keeping silent. For my part, I've been looking at that candle flame. Sometimes it trembles, other times it becomes brighter yellow, sometimes it pales. I don't know why this happens. But do we know, my sisters, why anything happens?…

(a pause)

The same. — To speak of the past — must be beautiful, if only for being useless and causing one to feel such pity…

Second. — Let us speak, if you like, of a past that could not have been.

Third. — No. Perhaps it could have been…

First. — You say nothing but words. It's so sad to speak! Such a false way of forgetting ourselves!… What if we were to go for a walk?…

Third. — Where?

First. — Here, from one side to the other. Sometimes this conjures up dreams.

Third. — Of what?

First. — I don't know. How should I know that?

(a pause)

Second. — This whole country is very sad… The one where I once lived was less sad. At dusk I would sit by my window and weave. The window looked out over the sea and sometimes an island appeared in the distance…

Sometimes I did not weave at all, I'd look out at the sea and forget to live. I do not know if I was happy. I will never return to what I may never have been…

First. — Away from here I've never seen the sea. There, from that window, the only window from which the sea can be seen, one sees so little!… Is the sea of other lands beautiful?

Second. — Only the sea of other lands is beautiful. The one we always see makes us miss the one we will never see…

(a pause)

First. — Didn't we say that we were going to speak about our pasts?

Second. — No, we didn't say that.

Third. — Why isn't there a clock in this room?

Second. — I don't know… But without a clock, everything is more distant and mysterious. The night belongs more to itself… Who knows if we would be able to speak like this if we knew what time it was?

First. — With me everything is sad, my sister. I pass through Decembers of the soul… I'm trying not to look out the window… I know that from there, in the distance, you can see hills… Once, I was happy beyond the hills… I was little. I'd gather flowers all day and before I went to sleep I asked that they not be taken from me… I don't know what it is that makes this feel so irreparable that it makes me want to cry… It was far from here that this could have happened… When will the day arrive?…

Third. — What does it matter? It always comes about the same way… always, always, always…

(a pause)

Second. — Let us tell each other stories… I don't know any stories, but that's not so bad… Only living is bad… Let's not graze even the fringes of our dress against life… No, don't get up. That would be a movement, and every movement interrupts a dream… At this moment I wasn't dreaming, but it softens me to consider that I may have been… But the past — why don't we talk about it?

First. — We decided not to… Soon the day will dawn and we will regret it… With the approach of light dreams fall asleep… The past is only a dream… Besides that, I don't even know what is not a dream… If I look at the present with much attention, it appears to me that it has already passed… What is anything? How does it move? How does it move from the inside?… Ah, let us speak, my sisters, let us speak together loudly… Silence begins to take shape, begins to be something… I feel it envelop me like a fog… Ah, speak, speak!…

Second. — For what?… I stare at both of you but don't see you right away… An abyss appears to be growing between us… I have to exhaust the idea that I am able to see you… This hot air is cold inside, in that part that touches the soul… I should now feel impossible hands passing through my hair… Hands through the hair — it is the gesture with which to speak about mermaids… (*She crosses her hands over her knees. Pause.*) Only a moment ago, when I thought of nothing, I was thinking about my past…

First. — I must have been thinking about mine too...

Third. — I no longer know what I was thinking... About the past of others, perhaps... about the past of wonderful people who never existed... A stream ran near my mother's house... Why did it flow further away or nearer?... Is there any reason for any thing to be what it is? Is there any true and real reason for that, true and real like my hands?...

Second. — Hands are not true nor real... They are mysteries that inhabit our life... Sometimes, when I look at my hands, I fear God... there is no wind to move the flames of the candles, yet look, they move... Towards where are they inclining?... What a pity if someone could answer!... I feel a desire to hear barbaric songs that must now be playing in palaces on other continents... there's always distance in my soul... Perhaps because, when I was a child, I ran after the waves by the sea. I took life by the hand between rocks, at low tide, when the sea seems to have crossed its hands over its chest and to have fallen asleep like a statue of an angel so that it would never again be seen...

Third. — Your words remind me of my soul...

Second. — Perhaps they do for not being true... I hardly know what I'm saying... I repeat after a voice that I don't even hear in a whisper... But I must have really lived by the seashore... I love everything about waving... There are waves in my soul... When I walk I lull myself... Now I would like to walk... I don't because there is never any point in doing anything, especially what you want to do... I'm afraid of the hills... It is impossible for them to be so still and enormous... They must have a secret made of stone that they refuse to reveal... If I could lean myself out this window for a moment without seeing hills, I could have felt happy in my soul...

First. — For me, I love the hills... On this side of the hills, life is always ugly... On the other side, where my mother lives, we used to sit in the shade of the tamarinds and speak about visiting other lands... Everything there was long-lasting and happy like the singing of two birds, one on each side of the path... The forest had no other clearing but our thoughts... And we dreamed that the trees projected another calm other than their shadows on the ground... It was certainly in that way that we lived there, myself, and I do not know who else... Tell me that this was true so that I don't have to cry...

Second. — I lived between rocks and peeked out at the sea... The hem of my skirt was cold and salty, beating against my bare legs... I was small and barbaric... Today I'm fearful of having been... The present appears like sleep... Speak to me of the fairies. I've never heard anyone talk about them... The sea was too big to allow one to think of them... In life it's nice to be small... Were you happy, my sister?

First. — I begin at this moment to have once been happy... Besides, all that happened in the shadows... The trees felt it more than I... The one I barely waited for never arrived... And you, sister, why don't you speak?

Third. — I am horrified to have told you what I am about to tell you. My present words, as soon as I say them, belong to the past, are outside of me, rigid and fatal, I don't know where they go... I speak, and I think of this in my throat, and my words appear like people to me... I have a fear bigger than myself. I know not how, but I feel in my hand, the key to an unknown door. And everything I am is a self-conscious amulet or shrine. It's for this that I'm afraid to move, through the dark forest, into the mysteries of speech... After all, who knows if I am like this and if this is really how I feel?...

First. — It's so hard to know how we feel when we become aware of ourselves!... Even life tastes like pain when we notice it... Speak therefore, without realizing that you exist... Were you not going to tell us who you were?

Third. — What I once was no longer remembers who I am... Poor happy girl that I was!... I lived among the shadows of the branches, and everything in my soul was trembling leaves. When I walked in the sun my shadow was cool. I passed my fleeting days beside fountains, I dipped the quiet tips of my fingers when I dreamed of living... Sometimes, by the lakeside, I'd lean over and look at myself... When I smiled, my teeth were mysterious in the water... They had a smile of their own, independent from me... It was always without reason that I smiled... Speak to me of death, of the end of everything, so that I have a reason to remember...

First. — Let's not speak of anything, nothing... It's colder, but why is it colder? There is no reason for it to be colder. It's not exactly colder... Why should we speak?... It is better to sing, I don't know why... Singing, when one sings at night, is like a cheerful and fearless person that suddenly enters the room and warms it by comforting us... I could sing you a song we sung in the house of my past. Why don't you want me to sing it?

Third. — It's not worth it, my sister... When someone sings, I cannot be with myself. I need to not be able to remember myself. And then my entire past becomes other and I mourn a dead life that I carry with me and that I have never lived. It's always too late to sing, just as it is always too late not to sing...

(a pause)

First. — It will soon be day... Let's keep up our silence... Life wants it like this... Near the house where I was born there was a lake. I went there and sat at the water's edge, on a tree trunk that had almost fallen into the water... I would sit on the tip and wet my feet in the water, stretching my toes below. Then I looked intently at the tips of my feet, but it was not to see them... I do not know why, but it seems to me that this lake never existed... Remembering it is like not being able to remember anything... Who knows why I say this and if it was I who lived what I remember?...

Second. — We are sad when we dream by the seashore... We are not able to be what we want to be, because what we want to be we always wish we could have been in the past... When the wave spreads and foam hisses, it seems like a thousand of the smallest voices speak. The foam only seems cool to those who imagine it as one thing... Everything is too much and we don't know anything... Can I tell you what I dreamed by the seashore?

First. — You can speak of it, my sister, but nothing in us forces you to tell it to us… If it is beautiful, I already sense the pain of having heard it. And if it is not beautiful, wait… speak of it only after having altered it…

Second. — I am going to tell it to you. It is not entirely false. Without a doubt nothing is entirely false. It must have been like this… One day I found myself reclining on the cold summit of a rock. I had forgotten that I had a mother and father and that I had had a childhood and past — on that day I saw in the distance, like a thing I only thought of seeing, a vague passing sail… Then it was gone… And when I noticed myself, I saw that I'd already had this dream… I don't know where it began… And I never saw another sail again… None of the sails of the ships that leave from this port are similar to it, even when there's moonlight and the ships pass slowly in the distance…

First. — From the window I see a ship in the distance. It may be the one you saw…

Second. — No, my sister; the one that you see, undoubtedly searches for some port… The one I saw could not be searching for a port…

First. — Why did you answer me?… It may be… I did not see any ship through the window… I wanted to see one and I spoke of it so I didn't feel sorry for myself… Tell us now what it was that you dreamed of by the seashore…

Second. — I dreamed of a sailor who had gotten lost on a faraway island. On this island there were a few palm trees, and vague birds passed amongst them… I did not see if they perched at any point in time… From the time he had been shipwrecked, the sailor had managed to live there… But since he had no means of returning to his country, every time he remembered it he suffered… He deliberately began to dream of a homeland he had never had; pretending that his was another kind of country, with other kinds of landscapes, with other kinds of people, and another way to pass through the streets and to lean out the window… Every hour he built this false homeland in a dream, and he never ceased to dream, during the day in the small shade of the great palms, which were cut out, fringed with peaks, on the warm sandy ground; at night, stretched out on the beach, on his back, not noticing the stars.

First. — What if there hadn't been a tree there to sprinkle my outstretched hands with the shadow of such a dream!…

Third. — Let her speak… Don't interrupt her… She knows words that the mermaids taught her… I fall asleep so I can listen to her… Speak, my sister, speak… My heart aches from not having been you while you dreamed by the seashore…

Second. — Year after year, day after day, the sailor erected his new homeland in a continuous dream… Every day he added a dream stone to this impossible building… Soon he began to have a country he had already traveled in. He already remembered having passed thousands of hours along its coasts. He knew the color of twilight in a northern bay, and how soft it was to enter, late at night, with his soul reclining on the murmur of ship parted water, in a great southern port where he had once been, perhaps happy, in his dreamed-up youth...

(pause)

First. — My sister, why have you stopped speaking?

Second. — One should not speak too much... Life is always watching us... Every hour is the mother of dreams, but we must not know this... When I speak too much I begin to feel separated from myself and to hear myself speak. This makes me feel sorry for myself and feel too much in my heart. Then I have a sentimental desire to have it in my arms so I can lull it like a child... Look: the horizon pales... Daybreak will not be long... Do I need to tell you more about my dream?

First. — Always speak, my sister, may you always speak... Do not stop speaking, nor notice the dawn of day... The day never breaks for those who lean their heads on the bosom of dreamed hours... Do not twist your hands. It makes the sound of a stealthy serpent... Tell us more about your dream. It is so true that it makes no sense. Just thinking about hearing you touches my soul with music...

Second. — Yes, I will tell you more about it. It is as if I needed to tell you. As I go about telling you I tell it also to myself... There are three listening... (*Suddenly, staring at the coffin, shuddering.*) Not three... I don't know... I don't know how many...

Third. — Do not speak like this... Tell us quickly, tell us again... Do not speak of how many are listening... We never know how many things really live and see and hear... Return to your dream... The sailor... What did the sailor dream of...

Second (*lower, in a very slow voice*). — In the beginning he created land-scapes; then he created cities; then, one by one, he created streets and laneways, chiseling them into the matter of his soul — one by one the streets, neighborhood by neighborhood, up until the ramparts of the piers from where he then created the ports... One by one the streets, and the people who walked along them and who looked over them from their windows... He began to encounter certain people as if he barely recognized them... He began to learn about their past lives from their conversations, and all this was as if he was only dreaming of the landscapes and seeing them as he went along... Afterwards he traveled through the landscapes he had created, remembering... And so he built his past... Soon he had another former life... In this new country, he already had a place where he had been born, places where he had spent his youth, ports where he had embarked... He began to have had companions of childhood and later — friends and enemies from his days in the sun... Everything was different from what he had had — neither the country, nor the people, nor his own past resembled what they had been... must I continue?... It causes me such pity to speak of this!... Now, because I'm telling you this, I'd gladly be speaking to you of other dreams...

Third. — Go on, even if you don't know why… The more I listen to you, the less I belong to myself…

First. — Is it worthwhile to continue? Should every story have an ending? Let us continue to speak… It matters so little what we say or do not say… As we watch the hours pass… Our purpose is as useless as Life…

Second. — One day, after it had rained heavily, and the horizon was more uncertain, the sailor grew tired of dreaming… he wanted to remember his true homeland… but he realized he couldn't remember anything, that it didn't exist for him… The childhood that he remembered was a dream; the adolescence that he remembered, was the one he had created for himself… All his life had been the life that he had dreamed… And he realized that it could not be that another life had existed… Neither a street, nor a person, nor a maternal gesture, could he remember… And of the life that he thought he had dreamed, everything was real and had occurred… He couldn't even dream of another past, or conceive that it had been different, as others had believed… O my sisters, my sisters… There is something, I do not know what it is, that I did not tell you… something that would explain all this… My soul freezes me… I barely know if I have been speaking… Speak to me, shout at me, so that I may awaken, so that I know that I am here before you and that there are things that are only dreams…

First. (*in a very low voice*). — I don't know what to tell you… I dare not look for things… How does that dream continue?

Second. — I don't know what the rest was like… I hardly know what the rest was like… Why does there have to be more?

First. — And what happened afterwards?

Second. — Afterwards? After what? Is there something after?… One day a boat came… One day a boat came… — Yes, yes… it could only have been this way… — One day a boat came and passed by that island, and the sailor was not there…

Third. — Perhaps he had returned to his country… But which?

First. — Yes, which one? And what happened to the sailor? Does anyone know what happened to him?

Second. — Why do you ask me? Is there an answer to anything?

(a pause)

Third. — Is it absolutely necessary, even within your dream, for there to have been that sailor and that island?

Second. — No, my sister; nothing is absolutely necessary.

First. — At least, how did the dream end?

Second. — It didn't end… I don't know… No dream ends… Do I know for certain if I am not still dreaming it, that I'm not continuing to dream, if I dream it without knowing it, or if dreaming it is not this vague thing that I call my life?… Don't speak to me anymore… I'm beginning to be sure of something, though I don't know what it is… They advance towards me, on a night that isn't this one, the footsteps of an unrecognizable horror…

Who would I have woken up with the dream that I told you about? I have a misshapen fear that God forbade my dream... It is undoubtedly more real than God permits... Don't be silent... Tell me at least that the night is passing, although I already know it... Look, the sun is rising... Look: the real day is here... Let's stop... Let's not think anymore... Let's not try to follow this interior adventure... Who knows what will be at the end of it?... All this, my sisters, passed in the night... Let us not speak more about this, not even to ourselves... It is human and convenient that we take, each one of us, our own attitude of sadness.

Third. — It was so beautiful to listen to you... Do not say no... I know it was not worth it... That's why I thought it was beautiful... That was not why but let me say it was... Besides, the music of your voice, which I listened to even more than your words, leaves me, perhaps only because it is music, discontent...

Second. — Everything leaves one discontent, my sister... Thinking men grow tired of everything, because everything changes. The men who pass on prove it, because they change with everything... Only the dream is eternal and beautiful... Why are we still speaking?...

First. — I don't know... (*looking at the coffin, in a lowered voice*) Why do people die?

Second. — Perhaps because there is not enough dreaming...

First. — It's possible... Wouldn't it then be worthwhile to close ourselves in the dream and forget life, so that death would forget us?...

Second. — No, my sister, nothing is worth the trouble...

Third. — My sisters, it is already day... Look, the mountains marvel at their own contours... Why don't we cry?... The one who pretends to be there was beautiful, and young like us, and like us she dreamed... I'm sure that her dream was the most beautiful of all...What did she dream about?...

First. — Speak quietly. Perhaps she hears us, and already knows what dreams are for...

(a pause)

Second. — Maybe none of this is true... All this silence, and this corpse, and this dawn are perhaps nothing more than a dream... Look well into all this... Does it appear to have to do with life?...

First. — I don't know. I don't know how it is with life... Oh, how you are stalled! And your eyes so sad, that they appear to be useless...

Second. — It's not worth being sad in any other way... Don't you want us to be quiet? It is so strange to be alive... Everything that happens is incredible, both on the island of the sailor and in this world... Look, the sky is already green... The horizon smiles gold... I feel my eyes burning, for having thought of crying...

First. — You cry with consequence, my sister.

Second. — Perhaps... It's not important... What is this cold?... What is this?... Ah, it's now... It's now... Tell me this... Tell me one more thing...

Why shouldn't the only real thing in all this be the sailor, and everything else including ourselves only one of his dreams?

First. — Do not say any more, do not say anymore… That is so strange that it must be true… Do not continue… Whatever you were going to say, I don't know what it is, but it must be more than my soul is able to bear… I'm afraid of what you did not get to say… Look, look, it's already day… Behold the day… Do everything you can to notice only the day, the real day, there outside… See it, look… It consoles… Don't think, don't look at your thought… Watch it coming, the day… It shines like gold in a land of silver. The soft clouds become rounder as they gain color… But what if nothing existed, my sisters?… If everything were, in some way, absolutely nothing?… Why are you staring like that…

(They do not respond, no one has stared in any way.)

The same. — What did you say that terrified me?… I felt it so much that I barely saw what it was… Tell me what it was, so that I, hearing it for the second time, won't be as scared as before. No, no… Don't say anything… I do not ask you this so that you'll answer me, but just to speak, to keep myself from thinking… I'm afraid of being able to remember what it was… But it was something huge and dreadful like the existence of God… We should have already stopped speaking… Our conversation had stopped making sense some time ago. That which is between us and forces us to speak has been going on for too long… There are more presences here than our souls. The day ought to have already arrived… They should have already awakened… Something is late. Everything is late… Why do things happen according to our worst fears?… Ah, do not abandon me. Speak with me, speak with me… Speak at the same time as me so that my voice is not left alone… If I notice that I'm speaking I'm less afraid of my voice than of the idea of my voice inside me.

Third. — Whose voice are you speaking with?… It's the voice of somebody else… It seems to be coming from far away.

First. — I don't know… Don't remind me of that. I must have been speaking with the sharp, trembling voice of fear… But I no longer know how to speak… Between me and my voice an abyss has opened up… All of this, all this talk, and tonight, and this fear — all of it should have ended, should have ended suddenly after the horror that you spoke to us about… I'm beginning to feel that I forget what you said, which makes me think that I ought to scream in a new way to express such a horror…

Third. — (*to the Second*) — My sister, you should not have told us that story. Now I am estranged from myself with horror. You were speaking and I was so distracted that I heard the meaning of your words and their sound separately. And it seemed to me that you and your voice, and the meaning of what you said were three different beings, like three creatures who speak and walk.

Second. — They are really three different beings, with their own real and individual lives. Perhaps God knows why… Ah, but why is it that we speak?

Who is it that makes us continue to speak? Why am I speaking without wanting to speak? Why don't we notice that it's already day?...

First. — Who could scream to wake us up! I can hear myself screaming inside myself, but I no longer know the willful path to my throat. I feel a ferocious need to be afraid that someone may now knock on that door. Why doesn't someone knock at the door? It would be impossible and I need to be afraid of this, to know what I'm afraid of... How strange I feel about myself!... It seems to me that I no longer have my own voice... Part of me fell asleep and is watching... My fear has grown but I do not know how to feel it anymore... I no longer know in which part of the soul one feels... They put the feeling of my body into a lead shroud... Why did you tell us your story?

Second. — I no longer remember... I barely remember telling it... It seems like it was so long ago!... Such sleepiness absorbs my way of looking at things!... What do we want to do? Do we have an idea of what to do? — I no longer know if this is speaking or not speaking...

First. — Let's not speak anymore. I find the effort that you make to speak exhausting... The interval between what you think and what you say hurts me... My consciousness floats on the terrified somnolence of my senses through my skin... I don't know what this is, but it is what I feel... I need to speak in long, hard-to-articulate, confusing sentences... Don't you feel that all this is like a huge spider who weaves a black web from soul to soul to bind us?

Second. — I do not feel anything... I feel my sensations as something one does not feel... Who is it that I am being... Who is speaking with my voice?... Ah, listen...

First and Third. — Who was it?

Second. — Nothing. I heard nothing... I wanted to pretend that I heard something so you would suppose that you were hearing something and I could believe that there was something to hear... Oh, what horror, what intimate horror unleashes the voice of our soul and the sensations of our thoughts, making us speak and feel and think when everything in us asks for silence and the day and the unconsciousness of life... Who is the fifth person in this room who extends their arm and always interrupts us whenever we're about to feel?

First. — Why should I try to terrify myself?... There is no room left for more terror inside me... I lean excessively on the lap of my feelings. I am completely submerged in the tepid sludge of what I suppose I feel. Something enters through all my senses that glues them together and veils them. The eyelids of all my sensations are weighed down. The tongue of all my feelings is tied. A deep sleep glues together the ideas of all my gestures... Why did you stare like that?...

Third. — *(in a very faint and extinguished voice).* — Ah, it's now, it's now... Yes, someone's woken up... There are people that wake up... When someone enters everything will be over... Until then let us believe that all this horror was a long dream that we've been dreaming... It is already day... Everything's about to end... At the end of it all, my sister, you alone are happy, because you believe in the dream...

Second. — Why are you asking me? Because I spoke of it? No, I don't believe in it...

> A cock crows. Suddenly, the light increases. The three watchers are silent and do not look at each other.
> Not far away, on a road, an empty car moans and creaks.

11/12 October, 1913.

FERNANDO PESSÔA.

THIRTEEN SONNETS

BY

ALFREDO PEDRO GUISADO

ASLEEP

Your hands slept in the lagoon of incense.
And through crazed, shattered avenues
My soul descended inside me seeking the mouths
That prayed for my Being over your vast mantle.

Vaguely descended into silence, panting,
Fighting in light, fluttering in the attack…
At night Egypt fell into my gaze,
In your crossed arms, tombs in Karnak.

Mouths of Pharaohs praying to weary mummies…
Thebes withers inside me in bronze echoes,
Fading into gray somber lamps.

Distressed, you sleep until
The swans in the lagoon are so whitened,
That they forge the Color of your slender hands.

EGYPTIAN DREAM

In the palace, the peacocks are only made of words…
The wings of the color of distance raised above me.
The peacocks exist… I feel myself seeing them…
And my dream of you, yonder, are lakes in the garden.

When I passed by in the park, I found Nitokris.
I saw her and stared at her hands in order to feel them…
My eyes were ships in worried waters,
My senses, rings on Nitokris's fingers.

Labyrinth of sounds. I fall into a golden sleep.
Dimmed anxiety. God descends my soul in gold
My eyes are meant to see you, arches in mirrors.

Prayers that I've never heard. Long drawn-out sighs
And your hands, far away, anointing divinities
Musing Ibis, pagans, over old carpets.

PAGAN

…Then I remember myself. I pray from a distance. I brood.
And the remembrance of myself is like my steps in the distance.
My own mysticism is arched in blue,
And I remain only Color over vanquished stained-glass windows.

Your breath is the light of old chandeliers
At the corners of the halls where I see myself pray,
And your footsteps of Pain are like smashing mirrors.
When I want to see you, you die in my eyes.

I hug myself crying. Your death is like seeing myself,
Gold wings in Tule, burning antiquity —
And having seen you dead, makes me fear losing myself.

I search for myself in silence and hear me in your steps.
Over pagan altars I rise up as a divinity
And Isis puts my Being to sleep behind loose curtains!

SEEING YOU

I stretched out my arms to embrace you
A door closed between us.
A scent of motherwort flew inside me,
A scene that allowed me to dream of you.

Your shadow departed through the windows
And got lost, far away, amidst the groves…
My fingers mused caravels,
Becoming extensions of your fingers.

I dream of you in a park of olive trees
Lifting you from the gold I burned
In the amphorae of the temple of my Being.

I see you despite your distance…
I moved away from myself to be a monk…
My eyes are the shadow of seeing you!

MAD PRINCESS

I see her pass in a curve of the road
A princess who went mad many years ago,
A princess whose Body is a spindle
In principalities of silk pheasants.

Her shadow, a blue lagoon,
Her hands weaving pine woods,
Remind me of ships reaching the pier,
Eagles without wings in a palace, in Tule.

Her fingers, nails that nailed Christ.
She looks at me from a distance. In her gaze I exist…
I pass through the prayers of an ancient mouth…

Dreaming, I arch myself over ivory.
I am an arch with which she plays in the garden
That princess who went mad many years ago.

BLIND HANDS

I

I feel that your hands are your vanquished eyes
Your eyes that in forgetting the prayers of the light
Become cloisters erasing the forgotten steps
Of God returning from shrouding Jesus.

I still feel fingers playing upon old violins,
Jumping in ropes of gold, in the afternoon,
Blinding you with sound. And your ancient gaze
Burns mirrors framed in candelabras.

Your fingers are oars striking your hands.
I still see in the palace rooms, panting,
Your hands of Pain half opening doors.

We search for ourselves in Color and when we are lost
Your hands pass through my fingers, musing
Ivory statues over the arcades, dead…

II

The strayed lions who guarded
The white staircase died. Old gloomy lions…
Of them there only remains the echo of their roars
Which the arches of the halls made more slender.

The laces you spun put mouths to sleep
And the wrinkles fell deep into your face…
At the end of the park, at night, the dying eagles
Guarded the shattered spindles in silence.

Long ago, you'd spin your dormant eyes.
You stopped spinning them and your eyes burned
In the color of your hands, in the cross of other sunsets…

Blinded from me, you left. And when you returned
Stained with Distance, my senses were
Palm trees which ran along the side of the road where you passed!

FORGETTING

The lakes sleep swans in the avenue
And the doors of the palace are closed.
Falling leaves, praying silk,
Dreaming of dead distant landscapes…

These landscapes were your chambermaids.
Flutes in the distance were your senses,
And your hands while unweaving dresses
Slept in the fringes of gilded skirts.

Your Shadow has lost its gaze…
I'm not sure if you're merely my own gesture,
A gesture of my long, cold fingers…

I do not know who you are… My forgotten eyes
Feel you inside me, asleep in my senses…
My senses, arches over rivers…

SALOMÉ

I

Salomé dancing over past mysteries.
— Dusk in dying bronze. Sunset in red veils —
Her senses, far away, were old ballets,
And her Body, dancing, was her senses.

Salomé dancing with her swarthy hands
That were silk halls, unclosing her robes,
And when She saw herself, she was her own breath,
And the Body in the ballet a mere curve.

Salomé dancing. — And the eyes that saw her,
Shut like lions for fear of losing her,
Lions drinking light from the light of her eyes…

I do not see Salomé. — Perhaps she is asleep…
Perhaps she is the painful Absence in my gaze…
Perhaps a pagan mouth kissing God's hands…

II

God, distant pier inside me, from where other ships taking sail
Lead my non-existence Away.
Dark-skinned Salomé dancing between stained glass windows.
Transposing her Feelings in Arch-sensations.

She stares into Anxious landscapes in her tired hands,
Landscapes dreaming of castles never erected.
And her lips run through her senses in a fire,
Musing princes–color descending from the arcades.

There is between Her and God the body of John.
And in her gaze, sleeping in a bronze prayer
The inclining of a palm is the shadow of the ballet.

Her Body still dances. And God in her dances.
Ballet-wings, far away, in embroidered chapiters,
God's gestures fall between frames of Soul!

DEATH OF SALOMÉ

The wax candles she had dreamed of were extinguished in bronze.
Raised in her Being, senses-mausoleums.
The palace, in the park, was a gaze of God
And the rooms of the palace were the ballets she used to dance.

She, fallen cup in an infinite orgy,
Vanquished Cup of Soul in remote canopies.
Her Body had been one of her ballets,
And her own Death was a ballet still.

Her hands were queens of empires
Where kings traversed with mysterious retinues,
Daggers of ivory raised in other hands.

Her Body, gold belt around her, sleeping,
A breath of God falling over missals,
Ash of Soul praying to another pagan Jesus.

REMEMBERING

I feel the colors, at night, being afraid
Sheltering in the shadow of your mourning.
I was king of the Goths, who, in Toledo,
The Tagus put to sleep. I'm still listening.

The rooms where I lived surround themselves with gold
Forgotten golden-grays, dormant gold.
And in my Soul, in which I am still king
I envision slowly falling thrones.

Sad pages seek me in the paths.
And my legend in scrolls of dreams
Silently writes my thoughts.

The domains that I lived in are other.
All the things that I once saw
Returned mystery to my gaze.

BEFORE GOD

When I saw you I became your flight
And I descended God to find myself in me.
I flew myself over bridges of ivory —
And one of the bridges, God, in my gaze!

I haloed myself with gold in cold shadow
And my flights fell destroyed.
My senses were God's fingers.
My Body was carried in Maria's lap.

Now I sleep Christ in pagan veils.
My hands are God's tapestries.
I return Longing to reach the heavens.

I rise even more. I'm the profile of Pain.
Upon the shoulders of God I look around
And God does not know which of us is God!

ALFREDO PEDRO GUISADO.

FRIZOS

BY THE DRAFTSMAN

JOSÉ DE ALMADA-NEGREIROS

JEALOUSY

Pierrot sleeps on the grass beside the lake. The swans next to him are thirsty and don't want to wake him while they drink.

A mischievous swallow as beautiful as all of them, soars close to the grass and playfully kisses Pierrot's nose as she passes. He wakes up and the swallow escapes, gazing backwards out of fear, should Pierrot, angrily, chase her through the fields. And the swallow wandered through the hills, but because he remained still, recharged in mischievous zigzags and mocking chirps. And her mocking chirps were very loud above him. Pierrot was already falling asleep, and the swallow in chilling descent landed two nipped sour cherries on his chest, and again he escaped.

Contented, he rose to his knees smiling, while his arms wandered far away, far away like the swallow that had escaped into the hills.

Suddenly he saw himself blinded — Colombina's exquisite fingers were playing with him. She lowered her fingers to his lips and exchanged through kisses the aroma of her perfumed palms. Then she hung a sour cherry from each of his ears, like carmine jewel earrings. They rolled in the grass and joined mouths, almost forgetting that they had them joined together…

— Do you know? The swallow…

And there he passionately recalled all the gifts of the bird. Pierrot spoke enthusiastically, looking at the hills, still in search of the swallow, and Colombina twisted her body in quiet pain and took his hands.

There was a white mask of pain on the grass, and the moon in her clear eyes had a sad look that said: Colombina is dead!

THE ECHO

It's very late. Is Adam coming? Where could he have gone?!

Perhaps he's out hunting; hoping to surprise her with a white deer from the forest.

It was dusk, and Eve was already feeling worried about the delay.

She called from the summit of the cliffs and heard another woman's voice also calling Adam.

It made her fearful: But judging it to be her imagination she called again: Adam? And again a woman's voice also called Adam.

She went softly back to the tent.

Adam had already returned and brought all the arrows, but there was no game!

He greeted her and threatened her with a kiss and she fled from him.

— Another other than She had also called for Him.

BROKEN PORCELAIN

The black Amazon was as beautiful as the sun and sad like the moonlight. Nobody believes it but she was a shepherd of greyhounds. Slender black figure, cypress searching for waves at the sides of the road.

On Autumn mornings, cold like the steps of a pool, it was She who released the gray hare to the greyhounds, and whichever caught it already knew with whom they would nap. The greyhounds wouldn't sleep on any other pillow.

On the grass, in the lacy shadow of the yellow leaves of the plane trees where the fountains of the washing pool spew tears of glass, the black Amazon dreamt of her enchanted Prince, and the greyhound of the day slept quietly, extending her snout in Her womb.

One turbulent morning the greyhounds all came back dejected, their snouts hanging — and none to nap with!

A sad flute was traveling along the way; ceaselessly crying out immense songs of weeping accompanied by funereal mute rattles.

The flute went quiet, a distant cypress moaned softly from the pains of the tattoo that was being cut into its chest. There, the shepherd remembered the name of her Lover. A gray rabbit and a twisted sling hung from his belt.

The greyhounds, like arrows, left the path open. And the rattles rattling…

MIMA FATAXA

She arranged him that rendezvous on the cemetery wall the day before. In fact, he had made his infatuated soul a slave to the blond queen of all the gypsies. He was Hers from the day when, following the roguish rhythm of her disjointed hips, he was bewitched by those white teeth sparking fire in the flint necklace. He felt the urge to bite those burning red fiery lips with kisses and the cheeks smoked from the fire of that mouth. And he wondered in his heart vanquished by the monotony of the shouts coming from the singing and roaring tambourines. She had bewitched him, that burnt-eyed tramp, fixing her braids at the bottom of the copper cauldrons where, while the sun shone, a smutty gypsy consumed his hours in boring hammering. That witch had enchanted him while sharpening her braids in her lips wet with saliva.

And in the dances the metal tick of the sandals, the babbling chatterboxes singing on the slabs, had a youthful tinkle; and the rattle-girdled wrists were a concert of yellow canaries glad in their cages.

And more beautiful than ever in the royal fountain, with her skirts rolled up, washing her legs in the dust of the road, exquisitely disordered, pulling up her very thick stockings, the color of red poppies, and tying a Gordian knot in a twisted white ribbon, mostly blackened, that she wore, like a garter high above the knee... And isn't it interesting that her dark skin wasn't caused by the sun, since her body was burnt all over. Whoever saw her climb the mulberry trees and strip them of the blackberries that made her lips and cheeks and fingers bloody, oblivious of the wind that lifted her skirts, would, like Him, put on a desireful smile and pretend to sleep under the lovely mulberry tree.

And on the way down, with her skirt raised like a basket, dizzy, half-drunk with too many blackberries, they would see her as beautiful as a woman is in a dream. And straddling the trunk she let herself slip slowly down but was forced upwards to a branch that was above. Then she hung on a hard branch, opened her hands, and plunged into the grass. And on her stomach, like a wallowing goat, she began to gather the scattered fruits. And her feline eyes, like a cat who plays with the white moon on red roofs, reaped more than blackberries.

THE SHADOW

(TRANSLATION OF A POEM FROM AN UNKNOWN LANGUAGE)

She also felt the desire to leave. What would she be doing there alone? The one who carries a spear, also carries a lady.

Her black shawl and deadly ill share a secret that come from the same light.

The years ran by without news and the girls died old from so much waiting.

And each night, on the shadowy bank, a slight silhouette, a tragic somnambulance drifts on and on, like a withered branch of cypress floating along the surface of the stream that gently carries it.

THE NAP

Hidden amidst the yellow of the sunflowers Pierrot peeks cautiously at her sleeping under the shadow of a tangerine tree. She too lowers her eyes, and pretends to sleep. Pierrot's white robes crawl silently through the yellow of the sunflowers. And because He comes closer, She pretends to sleep even more by unsoundly snoring.

Beside Her, unable to handle himself, he descended a silent kiss on her black open sock, airing her little foot. Then her round, smooth knees, and he was already bending over her knees, kissing her disheveled womb when She woke up tired from so much pretend sleeping.

And He threatens to flee, and She steals his escape in her outstretched arms.

Hurt by Pierrot's remorse, She caresses his face with great forgiveness. And after peace was made, it was agreed that She would return to sleep.

SONG OF LONGING

If I were blind I would love everyone.

It is not for you who sleeps in my arms that I feel love. I love my stillborn twin sister, and I love her by fantasizing her alive at my age.

You, my love, what is your name? Tell me where you live, tell me where you reside, tell me if you live or if you have yet to be born.

I love that white hand suspended from the side of the galley departing in search of other galleys lost at sea very far away.

I love a smile that I believe I have seen in the end-of-day light among hurrying people.

I love those beautiful women who indifferently passed me by and whom I never saw again.

I love cemeteries — the slabs are thick transparent windowpanes and I see naked virgins lying down in flower beds, beautiful women laughing at me.

I love the night, because in the escaped light the indecisive silhouettes of women are like the indecisive silhouettes of women who live in my dreams. I love the side of the moon I have never seen.

If I were blind, I'd love everyone.

RUINS

Ripped tambourines and lame crystal cups at the foot of the wall.

Ivy like Romeo, Juliet the battlements. And the wind touches, in distant mandolins, thin mute songs of dead princesses.

Sleeping dust, slender-handed white-haired noble granddaughter's minuets.

One night those battlements girdled endless sins; and still they guard the secrets of the silent kisses of many nights. And every night the old moon prays, crying: A long time ago there was a castle of noblemen in that place… And the moon, telling the story, stops for a moment — frightened by the underground cold.

One can hear dance rhythms and little silk giggles in the room that no longer exists.

Those ruins are the sacred tomb of a sleeping kiss — letters sealed with blue garters and golden clasps and royal blazons and *fleur de lis*.

Poor old ladies the color of moonlight, without a rosary or anything, and always praying...

Sleepless nights with the galleys on the sea and the soul in the galleys.

Muzzled archers in the night as the carriage returns to the palace through the King's park. Great hunting in the woods — white greyhounds and black Amazons. Red Knights and gold trumpets on top of the hills in search of two who are missing.

A gondola, offshore, and a page in the sands lifting up a lantern speaking the night's warning through the breeze.

Her shoe was untied in the sands, and they went to put it back on in the pits where no one is watching. The footprints of a kissing couple remained in the sand.

News of the war — cries inside, and black silk over the coat of arms. Candles burn, serpentines. There are hands clasped between flowers.

And the dark-skinned tower sings, lazily, twelve times the same pain.

SPRING

The sun is handing out golden alms to the fields.

The little warmed up shepherdess runs along begging for the shadow of the hunchbacked willow tree, a romantic poet with a passion for the fountain.

She takes a look at the fields, and the depopulated fields give her permission to be naked. How the light shivers as she cools off in the waters! Then she got out of the bathing pool for good and spread herself wide on the grass, drying herself off in the sun. But the wind coming from Azenhas-do-Mar brought sins with it. She felt the desire to kiss the son of Senhor Morgado. And then she remembered the kiss at the vegetable garden on the day of the fair. She closed his eyes to blind herself from the bad thought, and went on to remember Senhor Morgado himself at midnight as he entered the cellar. She shook her head to let the sin escape, but found herself in the vestry letting the Senhor Prior kiss her hand, and then her forehead... because God is good and forgives all... and then her cheeks and then her mouth and then... she ran away... She should not have run away... And now the miller, there in the village fair, dances with her and unintentionally, poor thing, goes to the mill still dancing with her. And she still remembers — sitting on the big trunk and someone else's hands loosening her garters and corset, while she listens to the sad story of the mill with fifty evildoers... She wants to remember more, let it be a sin! She wants more memories of the mill, but can't find any.

Ah! and when the drover, guiding the yoke, ran into her and asked if she had by chance seen a white butterfly, a very beautiful butterfly, flying all about, she denied having seen it, and the suspicious drover went on searching for it, even under her dress.

How she wished she could sleep with every one of them!

She knows not what she feels inside herself that teases her with well-being.

Had the white butterfly fled into her?

DARKNESS

In the daytime nothing could be seen, but in the evening one could see people approaching with daggers in their hands, slowly, quietly, rising from the pines and dying inside them. The daggers didn't shine: they were distant lights, they were strings of linen sheets draped from thin shoulders. And the breeze made broken winged gestures to the linen sheets, white egret wings fallen by hunting fauns. And the wind whispered new-born fears through the pines.

And Night came through the pines, it came barefoot with mute feet out of love for the noise, arms outstretched so as not to bump into the tree trunks and the night came blind as the lantern that hung from its waist. And it was dreaming. The shadows on seeing her hid their daggers in their empty breasts.

The moon is a golden orange on a blue Egyptian plate with unpaired pearls. And the black silhouettes of the pine trees lulled in the breeze were a ballet of dreamed up statues in azure windows. Shadow-thieving hands took the orange, and the plate mourned.

Among the thin pines, among the saddened pines, moans in the breeze came from the graves, and distant silent shouting — and far off, the thin pines, the giant pines, could hear them.

With all of them hidden behind the pines, the burning daggers crash into each other in the air. The bonfire is made, and the witches pray in a circle around them screaming litanies of Death. More witches arrive, bringing scythes and a coffin. My hair hurts, my eyes close and four angels take my soul... But the cicada, in a raucous voice, from beyond the hill, comes to tell me that everything sleeps in silence in the darkness.

The morning arrived like the day but nothing could be seen.

SONG

The young shepherdess died, everyone is crying. No one knew her yet everyone is crying.

The young shepherdess died, died of her loves. By the river a tree sprouted and the arms of the tree opened into a cross.

Her long hands no longer wave from afar. The shepherdess died and took her long hands.

Her laughing eyes no longer mock anyone. The shepherdess died along with her laughing eyes.

The shepherdess died, the flock is unguided. The flock without a guide is the shepherd's doom.

Where are her loves? There are gifts to give Him. No one knows if it's Him and there are gifts to give Him.

On the other bank of the river a saint came ashore from the high seas. She was dressed as a shepherdess to avoid being noticed. By day she was a saint, by night she was the moonlight.

The shepherdess in life was a beautiful shepherdess; the dead shepherdess is the Lady of Miracles.

THE TEA CUP

The moonlight faded further into a mask fallen on the embroidered mats. And the bamboos in the wind and the chrysanthemums in the gardens and the herons in the washing pool all commiserated with its end. The colorful idols and winged dragons fell asleep in a circle. And the geisha, transparent porcelain, like the shell of an Ibis egg, got tangled in a labyrinth just like the dragons of the gods in the days of Tears. And her slanted eyes, pearls of Nankim fading in the water, mingled, sparkling, through the gleam of porcelain.

He, in a final gesture, closed her lips with his fingertips, and said dying — To weep is no remedy; I only ask you not to betray me while my body is warm. He laid his head on the mat and died. And She, in an egret's cry, raised her arms high pleading Heaven for Him, and went strolling through the gardens, swinging her hands while all who passed her by looked at Her.

In the morning the neighbors came on tiptoes peeking through the bamboo, and everyone saw the squatting geisha fanning his dead body with an ivory fan.

This is shown in the picture on the saucer.

JOSÉ DE ALMADA-NEGREIROS.

POEMS

BY

CÔRTES-RODRIGUES

OPENING OF "THE BOOK OF LIFE"

Nublotic transcendences, rare metaphysics,
I modelled my Work with avaricious hands.
Liturgical litanies of feverish passion,
Twilights of sentimental fire burning,
Columns of Beyond-Dream, arches of commotion,
Cloisters of Arch-Sorrow where Thought
Lives far from the world, in deep adoration...

      Slender Castle
           On the river
           Of Love.
  I knighted myself,
  My warrior's spear shatters
         In the combat of Pain.

Architectonic theories of Beauty,
Transfigurations, resurrections, and Nature
In the long, sensory bottom of emotion,
Byzantian gardens where the Afternoon agonizes,
Fluidic aromas in mystic ascension,
Emanations of Love that the soul divinizes
In the Soul of another Soul — eternal communion...

      Unknown beach
      Of the sea of a life lived
      Where moonlight never comes,
      From where the ship of my Soul
      Departs on a calm night
      On the way to the Beyond.

And here is the great route followed in Me alone,
Departing from the world to reach the heavens,
Where You and I will go slowly
      From Life to God.

Lisbon — 1914.

NIGHTFALL

My sensations — boats without sails —
Wander from me. Purple sunset. I muse.
My eyes from Not-seeing-myself are windows
        Looking out over the abyss.

Abyss of Another Being. And the Hour cries
Nostalgic for Itself, but I, from seeing them
Wander from Being Myself, and the starless night
        Terrifies.

Delirium of purple agony. Prayer.
Tonight the sunset turned inwards. Darkness.
I disturb myself in sensation
      And fade inside myself
        And grow dark
The shadow of my Being is the solitude
        Of the day that died
        Was lost
     And will never return.

Lisbon — 1914.

AGONY

I raise my vacant eyes in the distance
     From the shadow of my Being…
They hover Beyond me, and my Yearning
     Grows tired of living me.

My spectral eyes of shock,
Eyes of Soul gazing at Themselves
Haloed with the endless light of the darkness
     Of the Life I lived.

Halo of Sorrow that ends
In the night of the abyss of my nothingness,
Silence, prayer, holy communion,
Dream of light that divinizes myself in You,
     Torture of my end,
          Soul anointed
          And lost
In the greatness of Itself. And already not seeing myself
Twilight Maceration of Me,
     I agonize from Being Myself.

Lisbon — 1914.

ALONE

The sea of my life has no distances.
Everything is water! The horizon
Merges with the sky. A procession of monks
Sinisterly marches over the bridge.

Lit candles, cloaks, litany,
And the river sliding into the sea,
And the girls arrive in the evening
Fetching water from the fountain without singing.

      White hermitage on the hill.
      Our Lady of Peace…

I returned a pilgrim without having been heard.
I tore my feet along the way.
Alas, the calm of all that lies
In cold forgetfulness! Over the bridge
The procession walks.
      Under the arch a boat sails calmly!
      On its way to the sea.
O lost vision of my Yearning!
I see myself alone in the dismal distance,
Corpse of my floating dreams.

Lisbon — 1914.

OTHER

I pass sadly through the world, oblivious to the world.
I pass through someone else's world, without seeing it,
Mystic, ideal, vagabond,
I feel my soul rise from the deep
      Abyss of my Being.

I live from Myself in Myself and for Myself
And for God in Me resurrected
I am the Longing for the Distance from where I came,
And I Yearn for the Distance in which
      I will finally be transfigured.

I live by God, in God and for God,
And my soul, forgotten somnambulist,
Staring at Him with its sad eyes,
Passes sad and alone looking at the skies
      Along the path of Life.

I was Other and, being Other, will remain Other
An other living the mystical beauty
Of the human form I embodied,
Of the tears of blood I cried
      In the land of sorrow.

Spirit purified in Pain,
Being who passes through the world without seeing it,
In this poor land of sin
Divine Love in God-induced ecstasy,
My Being is Non-Being in Other-Being.

Lisbon — 1914.

CÔRTES-RODRIGUES.

OPIARIUM

&

TRIUMPHAL ODE

TWO COMPOSITIONS BY

ALVARO DE CAMPOS

PUBLISHED BY

FERNANDO PESSOA

OPIARIUM

To senhor Mário de Sá-Carneiro

Before taking opium I'm twisted and spent
The feeling of life makes me convalesce and shrivel
The consoling of opium keeps me hopeful and civil
In an Orient east of the Orient.

This life at sea is killing me fast.
There are days when I'm feverishly ill
Despite my best efforts to adapt my will
I'm driven beyond the worst blast.

In paradox and astral upheaval
I live my life in golden creases,
Where waves dignify what decreases
And pleasures are the lymph nodes of my evil.

By a mechanism of disasters most rare,
A gear with fake steering wheels,
A walk between scaffolds reveals
Flowers without stems in the air.

In my inner life of lacquer and lace,
I stagger myself through my labor
Imagining that I harbor the sabre
With which the Precursor was unfaced.

I'm atoning for a crime in a suitcase,
My grandfather committed to live in plenty.
My nerves to the gallows go twenty by twenty.
I fell into opium as my birthplace.

To the sleeping touch of morphine
I lose myself in throbbing transparencies
And in a night full of shimmering errancies
The moon rises like my Fate unbefore seen.

I, who was always a student foregone
Do nothing at last but watch the ships sail
Through the Suez Canal bringing their mail
My life, camphor at dawn.

I lost those days I'd lived without check.
I only worked to feel my own harm
Which today in me is a kind of arm
That suffocates and supports me by the neck.

I was a child no different than others.
I was born in a Portuguese province
And I've met English people whom I need not convince
That I know English as well as my brothers.

I'd like to have my poems and novels
Published by Plon and in *Mercure*,
But it is impossible for this life to endure.
There aren't even any storms on my travels!

My life on board of sadness consists
Though I have a little fun now and then
Speaking with Germans, Swedes and Englishmen.
Yet the sorrow of living persists.

It's hardly been worth to the East to have travelled
To see India and China and Levant.
The earth all around is similar and scant
The one way to live comes unraveled.

That's why I take opium. It's my remedy
I'm a convalescent of the Moment
The ground floor of thought's my component.
Seeing Life go by is my enemy.

I smoke. I get tired. The land becomes whole
Where the west isn't far from the east!
Why did I travel to India to feast
When India exists in my soul?

I am disgraced by my gold.
The gypsies stole my Luck.
Find me a place before death is struck
To shelter me from my cold!

I pretended to study engineering by night.
I lived in Scotland. I visited Ireland.
My heart is a sojourning motherland
Asking for alms at the gates of Delight.

Don't arrive at Port-Said, iron ship!
Turn right, there's nowhere to mount.
My days in the smoking-room with the Count —
A French charlatan, lord of a burial's grippe.

I want to become things that can't be prevented.
I'm monarchical, not catholic, I know it.
Fated to become a somnambulant poet.
I return to Europe discontented.

I'd like to have beliefs and money to gloat
To be several insipid people I've seen.
Today, after all, I am nobody's queen
But a passenger on some lonely boat.

I have nothing that anyone seeks
The ship steward's more noticeable than I
With his upright manner and well knotted tie
Like a Scot *laird* that's been fasting for weeks.

I cannot be anywhere. My Homeland unbeckons.
I am where I am not. I am sickly and weak.
The ship commissioner is a rogue and a freak.
He saw me with the Swedish woman… the rest he reckons.

One day I'll make a scandal here on board,
Just to get people talking about me.
I can't bear life, the fateful decree
The overflowing anger I sometimes horde.

All day smoking and drinking predisposes
Me to American drugs that leave me frothing,
And I'm already so drunk with nothing!
If only they'd given my nerves a brain like roses.

I write these lines. It seems unthinkable
That while having talent I feel no charm!
The fact is that this life is a farm
Where a sensitive soul feels sinkable.

The English are made to exist unbeguiling
They are partners with peace and Tranquility,
There are none like them for stability.
One throws a Penny, another leaves smiling.

I belong to a generation of Portuguese
Who after India was discovered
Was left without work. Life all but smothered.
I've thought about this many times at my ease.

To hell with life and having to be dutiful!
I don't even read the book by my bed.
The Orient disgusts me. It's unfeeling lead
A mat that being rolled up ceases to be beautiful.

I fall into opium by force and deceit
One cannot demand that I live a clean life.
Honest souls who live without strife
Have plenty of hours to sleep and eat.

Damn them! And this, after all, is envy.
Because these nerves are my doom
If only there was a ship to transport my room
To where I want nothing that I don't see!

O come on! I would get too tired to budge.
I'd want another stronger opium to get me higher
To reach dreams that would destroy me in fire
And debase me in sludge.

Fever! If what I have is not a fever,
I don't know what it is to have a fever and feel it.
The essential fact is that I am sick and cannot heal it.
This hare, my friends, is a run-down disbeliever.

Night came. The first cornet like bad weather
Has already called us to dress for supper.
Social life above all! That's it! Scupper
Along until we're led out on a tether!

This ends badly. There's nothing to solve.
(Hello!) blood and a revolver there at the end
Of this disquietude that will not mend
And of which there is no resolve.

And whoever looks at me finds me banal,
Me and my life… Look! a boy…
My monocle alone makes me a toy
Hardly worth noticing at all.

Ah, how many souls there are just like me.
Straightened and mystical!
Under the coat of sophistical
Horrified by what life might be?

If only I was on the outside
As interesting as I am in the middle!
The vortex at my center's my riddle
To do nothing's the doom that I hide.

Useless. But it is just to be unmovable!
If only we could despise other persons
And even with shabby elbows or worse sins,
Be heroic, lovely, cursed, or inscrutable!

I want to put into my mouth both my hands
To bite into them deeply and meanly.
It would be a thing done obscenely
And distract me from other people's plans.

Absurdity, like a flower from that
India that I didn't find in India, is born
In my brain tired and worn.
May God change or end where my life's at…

Let me be here, in this chair or that,
Until they put me in my coffin.
I was born to be a Mandarin,
But lack the quietness, tea and mat.

Ah how good it would be to go from here
To the grave falling through a bursting trap door!
Life tastes like blond tobacco at core.
To smoke through life has been my career.

And after all, what I want is faith to be whole,
And not to have such confused sensations
Let God end all this! Open the foundations —
Enough with these comedies in my soul!

                    1914, March.
                    On the Suez Canal, aboard.

TRIUMPHAL ODE

In the painful light of the factory's big electric lamps
I write feverishly,
Gnashing my teeth, ferocious with the beauty of all this,
With the beauty of all this totally unknown to the ancients.

Oh wheels, oh gears, eternal *r-r-r-r-r-r*!
The strong spasm withheld from raging machinery!
Raging outside and inside of me,
Through all my nerves dissected outside,
Through all the taste buds on the outside of everything I feel!
My lips are dry, O great modern noises,
From listening to you too closely,
And my head burns from wanting to sing you with an excessive
Expression of all my sensations,
With a contemporary excess of you, O machines!

I gaze feverishly at the tropical engines of Nature —
Great human tropics of iron and fire and strength —
I sing the present, and also the past and the future,
Because the present is the entire past and all of the future
And Plato and Virgil are inside the machines and in the electric lights
Only because Virgil and Plato existed and were once human,
And traces of Alexander the Great, perhaps from the fiftieth century
Atoms that shall become feverish in the brain of hundredth-century Aeschylus,
Pass through these conveyor belts and through these pistons, and through
these wheels,
Roaring, creaking, whispering, thundering, clanging,
Giving my body a wave of exuberance in a single caress of the soul.

Ah, to be able to express myself as an engine expresses itself!
To be complete like a machine!
To be able to go through life triumphantly like the latest model car!
To be at least able to physically penetrate myself with all of this,

To completely tear myself apart, to open myself completely, to become penetrable
By all the scents of oils and heat and coals
Of this stupendous, black, artificial and insatiable flora!

Fraternity of dynamic totality!
Promiscuous fury of being part-agent
Of iron-and-cosmopolitan gyration
Of strenuous trains,
Of the ship's cargo carrier workforce
Of the lubricious, slow turning of the cranes,
Of the disciplined tumult of the factories,
And of the monotonous near-silent hum of the conveyor belts!

Productive European hours, wedged
Between machinery and useful tasks!
Big cities held up in cafes,
In cafes — oasis of noisy futilities
Where rumors and gestures of the Useful
Crystallize and precipitate
The wheels and sprockets and padding of the Progressive!
Soulless New Minerva of the piers and stations!
New enthusiasms for the statue of the Moment!
Keels made of smiling iron plates leaning up against the docks,
Or on land, raised, on the slants of the harbors!
International, transatlantic activity, *Canadian-Pacific!*
Lights and feverish wastes of time in bars, in hotels,
In Longchamps and Derbies and Ascots,
And Piccadillies and Avenues de L'Opéra entering
Straight into my soul!

Hey streets, Hey squares, Hey-la-ho *la foule!*
Everything that passes, everything that stops at the shop windows!
Merchants of every kind; overly well-dressed charlatans;
Obvious members of aristocratic clubs;
Squalid dubious figures; vaguely happy householders
Paternal even in the gold chain that runs across their vests
From pocket to pocket!
Everything that passes, everything that passes and never passes!
Overly strong presence of *cocottes*
Intriguing banality (and who knows what's inside?)
Of the petite bourgeois women, typically both mother and daughter
Who walk down the street with some purpose;
The false feminine grace of the sodomites that pass, slowly;
And all the simply elegant people who walk around and show off
And after all have souls inside of them too!

(Ah, how I wish I were the *souteneur* of all of this!)

The wonderful beauty of political corruption,
Delightful financial and diplomatic scandals,
Political aggression in the streets,
And every once in a while the comet of a regicide
That illuminates with Prodigy and Fanfare
The usual lucid skies of everyday Civilization!

Disproven news of the newspapers,
Insincerely sincere political articles,
Passez à-la-caisse, News, Big Crime —
Two of their columns pushed to the second page!
The fresh smell of letterpress ink!
The posters just put on, wet!
Yellow *vients-de-paraître* with a white girdle!
How I love all of you, everyone, how I love you all,
How I love you in every way
With seeing and hearing and smelling
And touching (what touching you represents to me!)
And with intelligence as an antenna that you make vibrate!
Oh, how all my senses are in heat for you!

Fertilizers, steam threshers, agricultural progress!
Agricultural chemistry, and the quasi-science of commerce!
O showcases of traveling salesmen,
Traveling salesmen, knight-errants of Industry,
Human extensions of factories and quiet offices!

O fabrics in shop windows! O mannequins! O latest outfits!
O useless items that everyone wants to buy!
Hello large department stores with several sections!
Hello electric ads that come and stay and disappear!
Hello everything with which things are built today, with which today is
                                          different from yesterday!
Hey, reinforced concrete, concrete cement, new processes!
Glorious deadly weaponry of progress!
Armors, cannons, machine guns, submarines, airplanes!

I love you all, everything, like a beast.
I love you carnivorously.
Wickedly and entwining my sight
In you, O great things, banal, useful, useless,
O fully modern things,
O my contemporaries, present and soon to come

Forms of the immediate system of the universe!
New metallic and dynamic Revelation of God!

O factories, O laboratories, O music-halls, O Luna-Parks,
O battleships, O bridges, O floating docks —
In my turbulent and glowing mind
I take you as I would a beautiful woman,
I take you completely as I would a beautiful woman one does not love,
Who one meets casually and finds extremely interesting.

Eh-la-ho façades of the big stores!
Eh-la-ho elevators of the big buildings!
Eh-la-ho ministerial recompositions!
Parliaments, Policies, Budget Rapporteurs,
Counterfeit Budgets!
(A budget is as natural as a tree
And a parliament as beautiful as a butterfly).

Hurrah to the interest for everything in life,
Because everything is life, from the shimmering stones in shop windows
To the night's mysterious bridge between the stars
And the ancient and solemn sea washing the shores
And being mercifully the same
As it was when Plato was really Plato
In his real presence and in his flesh with his soul within,
And spoke with Aristotle, who was not to be his disciple.

I could die crushed by an engine
With the delicious surrender of a woman that has been taken.
Throw me into the furnaces! Stick me under the trains!
Spank me aboard ships! Masochism through machinery!
Some kind of modern sadism and I and noise!

Up-la-ho for the jockey who won the Derby,
Biting your two-color cap between my teeth!

(To be so tall that I could not enter any door!
Ah, looking is a sexual perversion for me!)

Hey! Hey! Hey! cathedrals!
Let me break my head against your corners.
And be taken from the street full of blood
Without anyone knowing who I am!

O tramways, funiculars, subway lines
Rub yourselves against me to a spasm!
Hilla! hilla! hilla-ho!
Laugh in my face,
O cars crowded with bohemians and sluts,
O daily crowds of the streets neither happy nor sad,
Anonymous multicolored river where I cannot bathe as I'd like!
Ah, what complex lives, what precious household things!
Ah, to know about each of their lives, the hardships with money,
The domestic dissension, the debauchery no one suspects,
The thoughts that each one shares with oneself in their room
And the gestures one makes when nobody's there to see!
Not knowing all this is to ignore everything, O rage,
O rage that like a fever and a heat and a hunger
Makes my face thin and sometimes makes my hands shake
In absurd twitches amidst the mobs
In the streets full of jostling!

Ah, and the ordinary dirty people, who always seem to be the same,
Who use profanities as everyday words,
Whose sons steal from grocery stands
And whose daughters at eight years old — and I find this beautiful and love it! —
Masturbate decent-looking men on stairwells.
The rabble that walk on the scaffoldings and return home
Through almost unreal alleys of narrowness and rot.
Wonderfully human people who live like dogs
Who are below all moral systems,
For whom no religion was fashioned,
No art created,
No politics meant for them!
How I love all of you, because you are like this,
Your lowliness is too low to be immoral, neither good nor bad,
Unreachable by all progress,
Wonderful fauna from the deep-sea of life!

(In the noria of my backyard
The donkey goes around and around,
And this is the size of the mystery of the world.
Wipe the sweat with your arm, disgruntled worker.
Sunlight swelters the silence of the spheres
And we shall all die,
O somber pinewoods at twilight,
Pinewoods where my childhood was something other than
What I am today...)

But, ah again the constant mechanical rage!
Again the busy obsession of the buses.
And again the fury of travelling at the same time on every train
Throughout every part of the world,
To be saying goodbye from aboard all ships,
Which at this time are pulling up anchor and moving away from the docks.
O iron, O steel, O aluminum, O corrugated iron sheets!
O piers, O ports, O trains, O cranes, O tugs!

Hurrah big train wrecks!
Hurrah collapses of mining galleries!
Hurrah delicious shipwrecks of the great ocean liners!
Hurrah-ho revolutions here, there, and over yonder,
Constitutional changes, wars, treaties, invasions,
Noise, injustices, violence, and perhaps soon, the end,
The great invasion of the yellow barbarians across Europe,
And another Sun on the new Horizon!

What does all this matter, what's the importance of all this?
To the glowing red contemporary noise,
To the cruel and delicious noise of today's civilization?
All this erases everything except the Moment
The Moment with a naked torso hot as a stoker
The Moment, shrill, noisy and mechanical
The dynamic Moment when all the bacchants pass
Of iron and bronze and of the drunkenness of metals.

Whoa trains, whoa bridges, whoa hotels at dinner time,
Whoa appliances of all kinds, iron, brute, small,
Instruments of precision, crushing, digging appliances,
Drills, rotating machines!
Whoa! Whoa! Whoa!
Whoa electricity, sick nerves of Matter!
Whoa wireless telegraphy, metallic sympathy of the Unconscious!
Whoa tunnels, whoa canals, Panama, Kiel, Suez!
Whoa to all the past within the present!
Whoa to all the future already within us! whoah!
Whoa! Whoa! Whoa!
Utilitarian fruits of iron from the cosmopolitan factory-tree!
Whoa! Whoa! Whoa! Whoa-ho-o-o!
I don't even know I exist inside. I spin, I circle, I engineer myself.
They engage me on every train.
Hoist me onto every pier.
I rotate inside the propellers of every ship.
Whoa! Whoa-ho! Whoa!

Whoa! I am the mechanical heat and the electricity!
Whoa! the rails and engine rooms and Europe!
Whoa and hurrah for me-everything and everything, working machines, Whoa!

To climb with everything on top of everything! Hup ho!

Hup la! Hup la, hup-la-ho, hup la!
He-ha! Hey-ho! H-o-o-o-o-o!
Z-z-z-z-z-z-z-z-z-z-z!

Ah, if only I was everyone and every place!

London, 1914 — June.

ALVARO DE CAMPOS.

From a book titled *Arco de Triunfo*, to be published.

"ORPHEU"

LITERARY QUARTERLY

Copyright: ORPHEU Ltd   Editor: ANTONIO FERRO

DIRECTORS

Fernando Pessôa
Mario de Sá-Carneiro

YEAR I – 1915   N.º 2   April-May-June

CONTENTS

In special collaboration with the futurist painter

SANTA RITA PINTOR

(4 double hors-texte)

Publisher: 190. Rua do Ouro — Livraria Brazileira.
Printer: Tipografia do Comercio, 10, Rua da Oliveira, at Carmo — Telephone 2724

LISBON

To re-assert itself upon its *rentrée* "Orpheu" begins a long series of artis tic projects, the first ones being the following:

The Eiffel Tower and the Genius of Futurism, by *Santa Rita Pintor*.

Art and Heraldry, by the painter *Manuel Jardim*.

Futurist Theater in Space, by *Dr. Raul Leal*.

The Sphinxes and the Cranes: a study of psychological bi-metallism, by *Mario de Sá-Carneiro*.

EDITING SERVICES

Various reasons, both of an administrative kind as well as concerning the assumption of literary responsibilities before the public, have led the editorial *committee* of ORPHEU to consider it preferable for the direction of the journal be taken over by its present directors. This decision does not involve any disagreement with our comrade Luís de Montalvôr, whose collaboration, as a matter of fact, is included in the present volume.

❧ At first, the *ORPHEU* editorial *committee* had agreed not to include artistic collaborations: for this reason, it adopted the brilliant composition of the architect José Pacheco as its cover. Subsequent to the output of the first issue, the same *committee* determined, however, that it would be interesting to include drawings or paintings from **a single** collaborator in each volume, in view of which it was decided to **alter** the cover, removing its artistic character and giving it a simple and normal typographical appearance. The realization of this part of our program begins with the current volume which includes four definitive futurist works by Santa Rita Pintor.

಄ The *Manifesto of New Literature*, which was intended to be part of *ORPHEU* No. 2, is not included within the journal, nor does it accompany it. The reason for this is that the making of this manifesto involved the development of highly scientific and abstract principles. It will either appear with the third issue of the journal, or, perhaps, before it, in a separate booklet.

಄ The 3rd issue of *ORPHEU* will be published in October, with the delay of one month, — so that its active impact will not be hampered during the offseason.

಄ The *hors texte* by Santa Rita Pintor included in the present volume were photographed in the *studios* of the **Illustrators** according to the lithographic casting of

BARROS & GALAMAS

146, Rua da Palma — LISBON

CONDITIONS

All correspondence ought to be addressed to the Directors.

We invite all Artists whose sympathy is with the nature of this Journal to collaborate with us. Original texts that are not included will be returned.

Our trustees in Portugal are Sr. Monteiro & Co, Livraria Brazileira — 190 and 192 Rua Aurea, Lisbon.

ORPHEU will publish an uncertain number of pages, never less than 72, at the invariable price of 30 cents per individual issue in Portugal, and 1$500 reis in Brazil.

SUBSCRIPTIONS

(Per year — Series of 4 issues)

Portugal, Spain and Portuguese Colonies	1 escudo
Brazil	5$000 réis (weak currency)
Postal Union	6 francs

Livraria Brazileira de MONTEIRO & C.^{ia} — Publishers

190 and 192, RUA AUREA — LISBON

Just published:

SKY ON FIRE

NOVELLAS BY

MARIO DE SÁ-CARNEIRO

GREAT SHADOW — MYSTERY
MAN OF DREAMS — WINGS — I-MYSELF THE OTHER
THE STRANGE DEATH OF PROF. ANTENA
THE FIXER OF INSTANTS — RESURRECTION

1 VOLUME OF 350 PAGES

COVER DESIGN BY

JOSÉ PACHECO

Price 70 cents

UNPUBLISHED POEMS

BY

ANGELO DE LIMA

— Oh! Silent Night in Your Love!
— Oh! Scintillating Stars in the Night,
Like Ideal and Virginal Lovers!...
— Oh! Religious Memory of Love!...

— I once was... a Pubescent Child
That blooms into Unconscious Love
As in a Vague Dream... Movingly
A Scented Rose Blooms
— The Adolescent... Chaste and Curious!...

— I once was... the Gallant with the Refinement
To offer myself, Dodging, in Provocation
The Dangers of Cypressian Luck
— Sensory... In the Breeze, of the Oriental Sun...
— The Betrothed... Fearful and Desirous!

— And I once was... the One Engaged to the Lover,
The One Encircled in a Throbbing Embrace,
Anxe of the Inebriant Sacrifice!
— The Flower that Breaks the Gynoecium, Wide-Open,
— The Deflowered One... Grateful and Sore!

— Oh! Religious Memory of Love!...
— Oh! Stars Scintillating in the Night,
Like Ideals and Virginal Lovers!...
— Oh! Night in Your Love... Silent!

I once was... like the Lady, yes, during
Times of Comforting Bliss
In the Comfort of Home... Distant Today...
— As an Enchanted Palace is distant from the night...
I once was... a Virtuous Matron!...

And once I was... the Devotee of Love,
The Adulteress... who Betrays her Lord!...

And the one who felt Pain in her Heart
At the End of Too Much and Each Time
In each Attempt to Gather only Misfortune
In the Hopes of her Devotion!...

Oh! Night! Silent in Your Love!
Oh! Stars, Scintillating in the Night,
Like Ideal and Virginal Lovers!...
Oh! Religious Memory of Love!...

....

And if There Is in Love, a Chosen Love,
That, I also once was, who Nobody Was,
Who, in a Mystery, Hellish, Sweet,
Loved My Daughter, in her Bed...

Yes, if There Is in Love any Chosen Love,
My Sisters, Pull me close to Your Breasts
And Listen to this Painful Memory...

I Once Was the one who Lost Hope,
Who Wandered through Endless Nights in a Spasm
Between the Dreadful Darkness of the Jungles,
Anxiously in search of Lovers of Destiny...

— And the One who Remembered the Times of Childhood!...

— And I Once Was like the Shadow of Longing
Loving the Moon, for its Immensity!

— Oh Night! in Your Love, Silent!
— Oh Stars, in the Night, Scintillating
Like Ideal and Virginal Lovers!...
— Oh! Religious Memory of Love!...

NEITHA-KRI

O Night, Immensity of Immensities!
Receive My Confession.
I Never said no to the Truth!
Nor do I devour the heart in Remorse!...
I am the Great Queen Neitha-Kri...
I am a Devotee of the Thinking Night...
And Neith is the great Mistress of the Skies...
And I, Her Daughter, I am Nofrei-Ari!...

My Brother was King Mentha-Suf'reh!...
— He Died Rapt in an Ideal Dream
From a Philtre that I gave him to take!...
— Mentha-Suf'reh didn't Know Evil
— And Destiny Elected Me to Reign
Over the Miracles of the Country of Esneh!...

— I am the Great Queen Neitha-Kri!
— I am a Devotee of the Thinking Night
— And Neith is the Great Mistress of the Skies!
— I am the Queen!... I am Nofrei-Ari!...

— In My Divine and Perfumed Body
I have the Matte Color Flesh of Beauty
Which is Yellow in Color and Delicate,
The Blonde Color of the Ignited Flame...
— I have the Presence of the Ladies of Nobility
Consecrated in the Shape of my Body!...

— The Supreme Tiara that I Invested
Crowns My Haughty head
Royal, Sacred, Mystic, Proud...
— And then — O Neith — I am Divine within You!...

In the Shadow of This Crown of Thanitas
Yearnings of Hidden Desires
Beat in my Delicate Bosom,
Mysterious almost Undefined,
Even Knowing of My Veiled Gaze
— That you, O Night! in Your Love Excites...

The Sacred Breast Plate of Magic
Rests on its Enameled Gold
Cold on my Aroused Breasts,
Tacit-like, Oracle of the Day...

— Under the Hanging Pê-chênte around the waist
Over the gently Curved Vigor
Of my Thighs in Hieratic posture
That Burning Caverns and Love Dilate
In Fulgurous and Turbid Ardor...
From what Immanence... from which Immanescence?...

— O Night, my Mother in Immensity!
— O Great Night, Mistress Throughout the Heavens...

— Scintillating Stars in Her Solitude…
— I, On Earth, I am the Victor!…

— Raised in Curved Sandals,
I Stand before You, O Truthful!
Lady of Life, by Love Anointed…
Head Mistress Lady… Lady of Life!
I, Your Father-Mother! — the Ultimate…
— You Pass Between Waves of Incense…

— My Gaze is a sweet Fulguration,
As if in this Mirror of Truth
Of my Political Soul of a King,
— With that Foreknowledge with which I Know
— My loyalty was reflected
— Or the Light of Some Transcendent Star…

— And my Trembling Outstretched Arms,
Encircled in the Ritual Rings,
Fathers in the Palm of their Hands
Like the Keys to Reserved Seals…

I am Wiser than the Sages — I at last
— I who Know the Consecrated Secret
Of the Divine Filtering Lotus
Blooming in the Occidental River
Evoking the Absorbing Dream
Where Exiles Forget — the Evil Pain
The Home they Left Behind…
— Finding another Home beside Me…

— My gaze is soft Fulguration
In Sweet Profound Certainty
Like the Stars of the Immanescent Sky…
And Mother — O Neith-I! O more than Pure!
— Like the Stars in a Trembling Blaze…
— I am Serendipity, Daughter of Sorrow
Of That Longing Meditation of Yours…

— And just as the Fascinating Stars
Generate The Foretold Hours of the Instants,
— My Love – The Endless — breeds Madness!

NINEVEH

— Over There was — the Nineveh of Mercy,
The City of Peculiar Grief
And the Sepulture of Semi-Rami...
And Today... over There, Longing Wanders...
— And the Eternal Istar is in the Supreme Sky...
— And... The Serpent sometimes passes... — There!...

❦ ❦ ❦

In the Long Silent Chamber
Of Semi-Rami's Grave...
— Relegated from Glorious Life
      — To Mysterious Death's Final Peace
      — Cold and Homesick
      — Semi sleeps!...

— She died in the War in a Faraway Country...
— In the Fatal Expedition
In which three Million Soldiers died... — and even More...
— And the Faithful Guards of the One Who Had Been Triumphant
— Her One Hundred Immortal Guards...
In the Final Pity of the Last Tribute
Denoting Their Vigorous Bodies
— Sustaining over Willing Shoulders
The Sacred Coffin of Semi...
— Through Endless Lurid Paths
In Enemy and Jackal Lands...
— Through Suns of Fire... — Vast Sandy Landscapes...
— And the Sacred Terrors of an Oriental Country...
— They brought her Corpse from afar.
— And inhumed Her There...
— Cold and Homesick!...
— In the Long Silent Chamber
Of Semi-Rami's Grave!...

. . . . ? . . . .

—You were… in those Times… Before Time…
Your Glorious Gesture Generating Life!…
— And After Your Gesture…
— Supreme… Immodest…
— Grand and Tacit…
— Afterwards… Night in Immensity!…

❀ ❀ ❀

— And the Mother of the King of the South-Sunset Kingdom
Said to Mu-Ang — Once, perhaps…
— Look at the Clouds in the Sky… how it Runs!…
— Just like the Hours of My Bliss…
— Those who have Children on Earth — Don't Die!…
— If You Are King — Marry a Queen
— Equal to You In Greatness…
— And… After… Marrying Beauty
Then You Can Follow Your Own Pathway!
. . . .
— And the King Mu-An' said to the Queen, Then…
— Beside You… I am Enthralled in Charm…
— Removed, However, from my Country — For so long, —
That I don't even know if My Kingdoms still exist…
— I Return to My Kingdom… in Severe Pain…
— Let it be — The King's Mother's Mountain
Where This Grove of Trees Spreads Out
By the Lake… where We Are… saying Goodbye!…
— O Mother of the King… You overjoy me in the Heavens
— But My Heart Suffers in Secret!…

. . . .

❀ ❀ ❀

— How many from Chu-Si to Kuan-Su
— Sons of Heaven amongst Daughters of Kiang
— Consecrated in the Throne of Hoang
— Haloed by the Peacock Blue?…

SANTA RITA PINTOR. — Scientific one-head case + ocular apparatus + visual dynamic overlap
PARIS YEAR 1914. + ambient reflections × light.

(MECHANIC SENSITIVITY.)

— And Someday… They leant Peacefully
Over the Jeweled Table of Being Tame
— And they Closed their Eyes within Their Lashes…
— And they Lowered Their Quiet Gesture
Of Emperors of the Consecrated Empire…
— In the Gesture of Decency and Rest!

AND NOW THE FINAL GOODNIGHT… — MY SWEET!…

To my friends at ORPHEU

— My Sweet — Bird?! —My Soul?!…
— Blue Moth… — Trance!…
Who in winged labor, Wearies…
— Dormant in Peace… — Transpiercing Idea!…

— From Sunset through Epic…
Asleep… the Impetuous Body Tightens…
As it Goes to the Grave… — to Rest…
— My Sweet… — Bird!… — My Soul!!…

— My Heart Doesn't Ache For You…
— I Don't Cry, but Whisper in Prayer…
— In Profanity… — And Now… Elected!…

— Balm — the Grave — the Dew
That Falls over the Last Bed!…
— My Sweet!… — and Now the Final Goodnight…

ED D'ORA ADDIO… — MIA SOAVE!…

Aos meus amigos d'ORPHEU

— Mia Soave… — Ave?!… — Alméa?!…
— Maripoza Azual… — Transe!…
Que d'Alado Lidar, Canse…
— Dorta em Paz… — Transpasse Idéa!…

Do Occaso pela Epopéa…
Dorto… Stringe… o Corpo Elance…
Vae A' Campa… — Il C'or descanse…
— Mia Soave… — Ave!… — Alméa!…

— Não Doe Por Ti Meu Peito…
— Não Choro no Orar Cicio…
— Em Profano… — Edd'ora… Eleito!…

— Balsame — a Campa — O Rocío
Que Cahe sobre o Ultimo Leito!…
— Mi' Soave!… Edd'ora Addio!…

✿ ✿ ✿

— These Ancient Verses That I'd Sing
To the Beat That the Heart Makes
Will they be Remembered?… — They will be one day…
In the Gathered Scattered Memories,
In the Pious Devotion of Some Book of Forgotten Things?…
— Perhaps the One That Now Sings… Lives… Exists
Will Never Again Remember — Eternally?…
— And, Coming from Non-Being, Will, Finally,
Sleep in Nothing… Majestic and Sad?…

ANGELO DE LIMA.

MARIO DE SÁ-CARNEIRO

POEMS WITHOUT SUPPORT

to Santa Rita Pintor.

ELEGY

My satin presence,
All embroidered in pink,
You were always a goodbye in me
On a silent afternoon...

O long fingers that I touched,
But if I even touched, disappeared...
O mouths that I waited for,
And were never again stretched out to me...

My Boulevards of Europe and kisses
Where I was only a spectator...
— Such loose sleep my love;
— What gold dust, my desires...

There are hands hung from bulwarks
Rambling in my anxiety
All the moonlight ended in me
From the fairytale moon...

I was someone who was mistaken
Who found it more beautiful to have been wrong...
I kept the masked throne
Where I consecrated myself Pierrot.

My crystal sorrows,
My feeble regrets
Are today the old vestments
Of a heavy Cathedral.

Poor charms of carmine
That I had reserved for someday...
The blond, elusive shadow,
Will never draw me close...

— O my never written letters,
And my portraits that I tore...
The prayers that I did not pray...
Fake locks, flowers, and ribbons...

The "petit-bleu" that did not arrive...
The vague hours in the garden...

The ring of kisses and ivory
That never ringed those fingers…

Affectionate convalescence
In a white hospital of peace…
The hurt and doubtful pain
Of another time more lilac…

An arm that soothes us…
Colorful books at the bedside…
My frigid tenderness —
To have nursemaids for life…

O great universal Hotel
Of my frantic mistakes,
With central heating,
Rogues, cocottes, gypsies…

O my Cafes teeming with life
And multicolored dancers…
— Oh, my sorrows are no more
Than their interrupted dance.

Lisbon – March 1915

MANUCURE

The sensation of polishing my nails,
Creates a sudden inexplicable feeling of tenderness,
I am fully included in Myself — piously.
And yet, here I am alone in the Cafe:
In the morning, as always, in yellow yawns.
Only the tables around me — ungrateful
And hard, cornered in their loutish,
Quadrangular and free-thinking ungracefulness…
Outside: a light and sunny day in May
A brutish day — provincial and democratic
That my delicate, refined, slender urban eyes
Cannot tolerate — but only strenuously
Support with nausea. All my sensitivity
Takes offense at this day that shall have singers

Among the friends I sometimes spend time with —
Swarthy, natural, with full-moustaches
Who write but belong to political parties
And attend republican congresses,
Visit easy women, enjoy red wine,
Pears and fried sardines...

And I, always in the sensation of filing my nails
And painting them with a Parisian polish,
Become more and more tender
Until I weep for Myself...
A thousand colors in the Air, a thousand throbbing vibrations,
Misty diverted plans
Knocking down arrows, volatile lists, flexible discs,
They arrive and line up before me tenuously
All the tenderness that I could have lived
All the greatness that I could have felt,
All the scenarios which I meanwhile Was...
This is how, little by little, I focus myself
On the feeble obsession of a smile
Which vague mirrors reflected...
Light sinusing inflection...
Fine crystalized shiver...
Unattainable displacement...
Fast atmospheric spark...

And everything conducted me through space in this way
Through innumerable intersections of plans
Multiple, free, sliding.

It is there, in the great Mirror of ghosts
That my entire past undulates and entangles,
And my present collapses,
And my future is already dust...
....

I lay down my files,
My scissors, my bottles of varnish
The polishers of my sensation —
And let my eyes go mad from Air!
Oh! To exhaust all that is embedded in it,
To flog its Beauty — without support, at last! —
To sing of what it revolves, shapes, impregnates,
Spreads and expands in vibrations:
Subtilized, successive — perpetual to Infinity!...

The hubcaps suspended between vaulted ceilings of ruins,
The solid broken triangles through the naves!
The propulsions behind vertical flight!
The graceful spheres succeeding a tennis ball! —
The blond oscillations that the player's mouth smiles...
The red garlands, what fans, when the Russian dancer,
Half-naked, shakes the painted hands of Salomé
On a great stage of Gold!
—May you surrender other dances!

Ah! But such inflections of precipice, shrill, blinding,
The brutal, diverging vertices, creaking,
Intersecting Apache knives
High cold dawns...

And through the stations and loading docks,
The great accumulated crates,
The suitcases, the bundles — pêle-mêle...
All inserted in Air,
Grown fond of it, separated by it
In multiple interstices
Where I feel my Soul wander off!...

— Oh futuristic beauty of commodities!

— Fabrics for sacks,
How I wish I could wear You like a toga!
— Wood for crates,
How I long to stick my teeth into You!
And the nails, the ropes, the hoops... —
But, above all, how they dance sparkling
To my audacious eyes of beauty,
The inscriptions of all these bundles —
Black, red, blue, or green —
Today's Shouts and Trade & Industry
In cosmopolitan transit:

FRAGILE ! FRAGILE !

843 — AG LISBON

492 — WR MADRID

Hungry for the new atmospheric Beauty,
My gaze meanders in the constant frenzy of absorbing
It around me. And with what magic, in truth, everything is shaken.
By the great insidious fluid,
Turns, grotesquely — swift,
Imponderable, slender, frivolous…
Look at the tables… Hey! Hey!
There they go, gamboling about in the Air,
In an instantaneous series of squares
There — but already further, in deviating diamonds…
And the rows are indistinguishably intertwined,
And the tables are intermingled with garish insinuations
From the red velvet counters
Which flank the whole Cafe…
And, higher, in oblique planes,
Aerial symbolisms of faint heraldry.
Dazzle the checkers of straw seated chairs
Which in their groggy horizontal sleep
Finally rise in the saraband…

My eyes anointed with Newness,
Yes! — my futurist eyes, my cubist eyes, my intersectionist eyes,

They won't stop quivering sipping and sparkling
All the spectral, transferred, substitute beauty,
All this Beauty without Support,
Disjointed, immersed, always variable
And free — in continuous mutations,
In unfathomable divergences…

— What about my banal porcelain cup?
Ah, how it exhausts itself in Greek amphora curves,
Ascending in a vortex of spirals
That its friezed brim emits in gold…

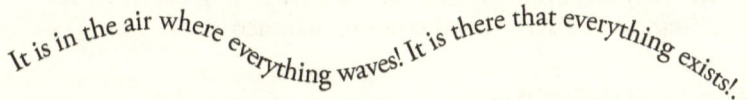

It is in the air where everything waves! It is there that everything exists!…

…From the long clear windows that look over the street,
Now, theories of hyaline vertices arrive
Throbbing foggy and diffuse crystallizations.
As a ray of sunshine passes through the larger window,
Knots, scribbles, arrows, aces — in the multicolored dust —.
Dance in space dyeing it in fantasies.

APOTHEOSIS.

....

A tone resounds beside me:
Sonorous hints!
This was what was missing in the landscape...
Acoustic waves make it still more subtle:
There they go! There they go! Look how well they run!
There they sneak delicately, splendor does of Soul...

A voice on the phone asks for a number:
North — 2, 0, 5, 7...
Casts of algorithms nailed to the Air:

Ascension of Numerical Beauty!

$$1.3.4.5.6 \quad 7 \; 7_{\,7} \quad {}^{8\;8}_{\;\;0}{}_{2} \quad {}^{4}_{1\;3}{}^{1\;4} \quad 5\;9\;6 \quad {}_{1}{}^{1}{}_{1}{}^{1} \quad 5\;5{}^{0\;0} \quad {}^{\infty}_{\;\;\infty}{}^{\infty} \quad {}_{\infty \quad \infty}$$

In the distance, a servant drops a tray...
Endless wonder!
A new whirlwind of silvery waves
Extends into circular lustrous, rustling echoes,
Like cold water sprinkling and cooling the environment...

— My eyes exhausted by Beauty!

Ineffable shadowy daydream —
My eyelids lowered in a glimpse...

....

...I begin to remember Jade rings
On certain hands that I once possessed —
And here they are, through magic, already entwining the Air...
Reminding me of kisses — and crimson marquetry...

Spangled propellers diverge...
Crests open, edges split...
Small sounds of gold interlock themselves...
Spires lifted, crosses locked...
Stars splintered, feathers fall...

In soreness, I turn my eyes from this wealth
and shut them fiercely...

In vain! There is no defense:
A host of plans are lashed to my ears,
Amidst the darkness —
Plans, intervals, breaks, jumps, slopes…

— Oh theatrical magic of the atmosphere
— Oh contemporary magic — only us,
Those of the present, bent you and shake you!

. . . .

Whoa! Whoa!
The throng of vibrations sail
Like never before, consuming themselves in iridescent rhythms!
I feel myself being transmitted through the air, in yarns!
Whoa! Whoa! Whoa!…

(How everything is different
Unrealized in gas:
Having been free-thinkers, the fluid tables,
Diluted,
Are now, like me, Catholic, like me, monarchical!…)

. . . .
. . . .

Serene.
A foreigner sits in front of me
Unfolding the "Matin".
My eyes, already calm in space,
As they glimpse the characters from a distance
Begin to vibrate
The new typographical sensitivity.

Eh-la! thick Normand headlines in sensation!
Tapered Italics of the daily chronicles!
Roman font-12, comfortable and bourgeois!
Gothic, cursive, round, English, capitals!
Miniature type for the small advertisements!
My elzevir of pederastic curves!…
And the typographic ornaments, the vignettes,
The thick black borders,
The frivolous "puzzle" of punctuation,

The asterisks — the inverted commas… the accents…
Eh-la! Eh-la! Eh-la!

T S A b c ⋰ ⊼ (q̃)   Y   ! Z ◦ ⤸ A w Δ ũ Ω
o . ϰ q̃ ẽ < ＊ … &' ;   ＊ ẽ Θ - > ũ " — ã §
P ⤸ W s β ~ Λ " "   O ⲍ ? õ x Φ F i & Π

— Ancient and modern alphabets,
Greek, Gothic,
Slavic, Arabic, Latin —,
Hiya-ho! Hiya-ho! Hiya-ho!…

(Hip! Hip-la! New onomatopoeic friendliness
Reminiscent of pure alphabetic beauty:
Uu-um… kess-kresss… vliiim… tlin… blong… flong… flak…
Pa-am-pam ! Pam… pam… pum… pum… Hurrah!)

But the foreigner turns the page,
He reads the Breaking News,
As light as the page from the newspaper,
In a twirl of letters,
All the world rests in his hands!

— Hurrah! for you, typographic industry!
— Hurrah! for you, journalistic enterprises!

MARINONI LINOTYPE

O SECULO BERLINER TAGEBLATT

LE JOURNAL LA PRENSA

CORRIERE DELLA SERA THE TIMES

NOVOÏÉ VREMIÁ

At last, the advertisement page unfolds…

— The zebraesque emotionality of Advertisements
Oh futurist — up-to-date aesthetic of commercial brands,
Of firms and signboards!…

LE BOUILLON KUB

VIN DÉSILES

PASTILLES VALDA

BELLE JARDINIÈRE

**FONSECAS,
SANTOS & VIANNA**   HUNTLEY & PALMERS   **"RODDY"**

Joseph Paquin, Bertholle & C.ie

LES PARFUMS DE COTY

SOCIÉTÉ GÉNÉRALE

CRÉDIT LYONNAIS

BOOTH LINE   NORDDEUTSCHER LLOYD

COMPAGNIE INTERNATIONALE DES WAGONS LITS ET DES GRANDS EXPRESS EUROPÉENS

And the svelte simplicity of the firms, LIMITED.

．．．
．．．

All this, however, all this, I again endow to the Air
Since all this Beauty waves there too:

Numbers and letters, firms and billboards —
High-reliefs, ornamentation!...—
Words in freedom, wireless sounds,

MARINETTI + PICASSO = PARIS < SANTA RITA PIN-

TOR + FERNANDO PESSOA

ALVARO DE CAMPOS

! ! ! !

Before I get up I remember something,
The Parisian wonder of zinc counters,
In the bars... I don't know why...

— Un vermouth cassis... Un Pernod à l'eau...
Un amer-citron... une grenadine...

....
....
....

I get up...
— Defeat!
In the back in greater excess, there are mirrors that reflect
Everything that oscillates through the Air:
More beautiful through them,
More subtly highlighted...
— O unfastened dream, O errant moonlight,
I will never be able to sing,
As I yearned to, until the spasm and the Gold,
All this unattainable Beauty,
This pure Beauty!

I roll away from myself down a staircase...
My hands clenched,
I completely forget the idea that I painted them...
And with grinding teeth, eyes diverted,
Without a hat, like one possessed:
I make up my mind!

Then I run to the street prancing around and screaming:

— Hilá! Hilá! Hilá-hô! Eh! Eh!...

Tum... tum... tum... tum tum tum tum...

V L I I I M I I I I M ...

BRÁ-ÔH ... BRÁ-ÔH ... BRÁ-ÔH! ...

FUTSCH! FUTSCH! ...

ZING-TANG ... ZING-TANG ...

TANG ... TANG ... TANG ...

PRÁ Á K K! ...

Lisbon — May 1915.

MARIO DE SÁ-CARNEIRO.

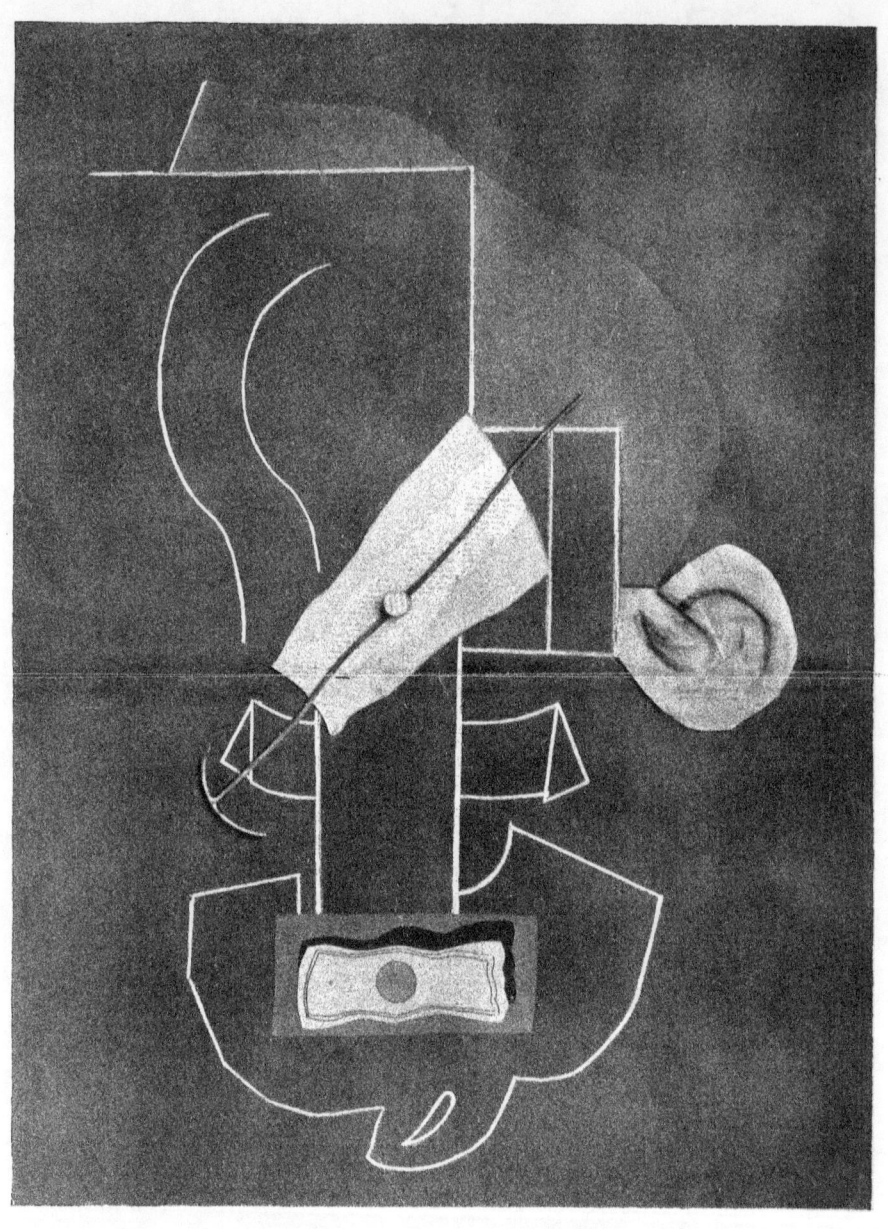

SANTA RITA PINTOR. — Static interpenetration of a head – absolute congenital
PARIS YEAR 1913.   complementarity

(LITHOGRAPHIC SENSITIVITY.)

POEMS

BY

EDUARDO GUIMARAENS

ON THE SWAN OF STÉPHANE MALLARMÉ

A dream exists in us like a swan on a lake
of deep and clear water at the bottom of which
there exists another white swan even whiter and sadder
than the real form of its sorrowful and vague tone.

Nothing: and its movements, of caresses and fondling,
reminiscent of the tenuous image, where sadness insists
on being whiter, the inverse grace that consists
in the sorrowful silence of a prophetic mirror.

A Swan exists inside us like a calming dream,
placid, a white and sad Swan, long and loose
and pure, the hidden side of our soul.

And its image resembles the image of a destiny
of purity and love that follows, step by step,
this immortal Dream like a divine Swan.

DEAD LEAVES

From this Belgian clock, enormous, white and sad,
the hours topple like dead leaves.
During an autumn afternoon, spleenlike sadness and dead leaves:
In each black vase there is a sad and noble lily.

In each black vase there is a sad and noble lily
and the hours topple like dead leaves.
Why was I not born a noble and sad lily,
An unfragrant petal amidst these dead leaves?

A Versailles sparkles in each sad illusion,
an autumnal Versailles carpeted with dead leaves!
In each black vase there is a sad and noble lily
and the hours topple like dead leaves…

UNDER YOUR TEARLESS EYES

Ah! Surely you won't say
that I did not love you, that I did not suffer!
— To me your soul was like a deserted
hall where, one night, I lost myself.

A bouquet of violets withered
on each piece of furniture shrouded in dust;
the purple of the curtains, ruddy, shuddered
tied to every window. I hesitated, alone.

— And my heart, almost wounded by you,
the childlike doubt that had already muted it,
was an old sleeping piano
that nobody will ever wake up.

EDUARDO GUIMARAENS.

ATELIER

—

A VERTIGINOUS NOVEL

BY

RAUL LEAL

Atelier

———

In waves of strange perfumes, convulsive exhalations of Dream vaguely illuminate the artist's dark lair. There is no other light. A few steps away from a canvas, as deep as the pain it evokes through the vibrations of a sinister hallucination, the model vigorously contorts his soul, revealing in his countenance the torture that his soul seeks. He understands art. In his spirit he feels the expression of beauty dragging him as he anxiously strives to convey to the artist the sublime inspiration of breathtaking pain. In his own physiognomy he idealizes it, torturing the spirit that only then, in his semblance comes true… through pain! His gigantic personality sacrifices everything to beauty, as it depends on beauty to live!…

Wrapped in the convulsive darkness that his spirit conceives, Moonlight ardently exudes the delirium of death, the eternal spasm of Existence that only he can feel, and it is in this environment of horror that he vigorously concentrates on himself, supreme synthesis of the Universe. It is in this environment, strong and sublime, that Moonlight, the ideal model, seeks to eternally devastate life!… And the horror that his soul becomes, he dominates and… vigorizes…!

It grows at that moment from a tragic art that matter hardly touches, in which only the spirit vibrates in transcendent vibrations that barely materialize through sensation. It grows in these instants, insensitive to the vulgar life that does not conceive the interior of things, totally unaware of the convulsive spiritualism of Existence in a strange unconsciousness. The sublime madness of spirit grows in the soul of Moonlight which the dark, immaterial vertigo of the Universe, deliriously accentuates in a divine tragedy of Life. The fiery transcendentalism of Yearning painfully expresses the spasmodic hysteria that Existence forms, by the convulsive rapture of the Universal Dream!… And in

these instants everything in him vibrates, all that is of the Spirit… Feeding on
his tragic conception, and thus on his soul, which becomes the soul of Existence!

In the atelier of the painter Moonlight vigorously prepares the soul, thus
preparing the expression of his semblance. And it becomes sublime, reaching
the vertigo of the Infinite… Through his delirium, the convulsive dream
sweeps him all away, awakening the artist who is thus totally sublimated too!
Moonlight is the very inspiration that the artist etherizes…

In an impetuous crescendo the dream that Moonlight fully becomes, fully
emerges in the genius of the painter, and thus the artist, in whom the dream is
vaguely blurred, is finally lost, elated in the same ideal diaphanous atmosphere,
tragically divinizing the soul!… Everything is ethereal and deeply convulsive;
a vibrant hallucination transforms everything, enrapturing everything in its
whirlwind genius…! A powerful mediumistic action then provokes the total
levitation of things, thus etherized… And Moonlight is the dark focus of the
sinister hallucination that fades out all around!…

In the vibrant rapture in which the soul of Moonlight drags everything
with it, a growing passion is strongly sketched, and it is that passion that shakes
the genial personality of the model all over, in the convulsions of flesh fully
expressing itself, in sobbing waves of longing spread impetuously through the
nebulous ether wholly lost in the mansion of the artist!… The growing passion
that enraptures everything and that wants to enrapture everything becomes
formidable… Like infernal elves that barely outline themselves, the sickly
conception of Moonlight vertiginously generates ephemeral shadows. And
everything that can still hurt the senses struggles convulsively in a paroxysm
of madness like a vast swirling of all the expressions of pain that only a vigorous soul could conceive! Yes, everything in the soul of Moonlight transforms
and he ardently wants to transform everything…! He wants transformation,
enrapturing everything in his spirit!…

His soul works for the artist. The artist, in his conception divinizes himself…! He is the vibrating reflection of his dream, of the dream that forms
him, in which he convulsively etherizes himself… He becomes the supreme
emanation of his soul!… Only the inspiration sublimates him, personalizes
him — and the inspiration is Moonlight!

Moonlight, full of yearning wants to preserve in his spirit, that strange
being that he himself created as he spills his soul generously onto the canvas,
and his ardent passion, the passion of pain, transforms into waves of pleasure
like bonds of hell. And he throws them to the artist who, in a whirlwind of fire,
the fire of his passion, wants to enrapture his soul more fully!… An intimate,
obscure struggle is generated! Impetuous are the convulsions of spirit that,
emanating from Moonlight, completely shake up the personality of the artist.
In the artist they appear faint, losing themselves through space, a diaphanous
brightness of infinite light!… And Moonlight senses this and almost lets loose
his own Dream, come to life in the imagination of the painter… for the fear
of an alien victory! His own inspiring force terrifies him. If indeed the artist
did not let himself become enthralled by Moonlight's dream, would he not

find himself in a vague spiritual etherealization?… No and, therefore, any overwhelming force, from ill-brought Moonlight, would not abruptly make him crash into matter in which he would remain, and which habit would then render almost insensitive. Moonlight fears being misunderstood. If all his passion for the artist unleashed in a supreme debauchery, a paroxysm of art, the artist, who has not yet attained that paroxysm, who is simply a reflection of the inspiring focus, a mere unstable nebula, a simple irradiation of the dream in which he vaguely bathes, might fall away forever from the soul of Moonlight in a fatal crash. But the yearning is equally strong, the yearning to complete the evolution of the artist in the dark focus of his soul!… And yet, Moonlight does not yet possess the infinite force, his strength fades, he does not contain the continuity of the Infinite… Art, in its lush spasmodic paroxysm of pain, still in the soul of the artist — is defined, concretized in images. He only conceives the image, he does not conceive of the Spirit, the Absolute Indefinite that in a debauchery of spirit would be vertiginously unleashed!… And perhaps the vigor of a transcendent lust and the savage material brutality confuse the artist, crashing from the diaphanous dream which, emanating from Moonlight, is only outlined in himself?

At last Moonlight wants to enrapture the artist, by totally internalizing him in himself through convulsive debauchery — he ardently longs for this, but fear makes him hesitant, the fear of being misunderstood, of being considered a mere animal full of heat, and finally, of losing forever the soul to which he so much aspires!… He fears his strength and his weakness, his strength which, by a cruel illusion, may unfold the horror of matter before the artist elevated above it, thus showing it to be contemptible. His weakness can no longer raise the artist to the paroxysm of art that is the paroxysm of debauchery and… pain!… And while the artist admires Moonlight, he does not feel him, nor merge into the convulsions of his soul… How we admire what is foreign to us, only feeling what we no longer admire.

The anguish in which Moonlight struggles is horrible. He has never dreamed of a pain like this! Like rags of dark clouds in a macabre dance, vague and obscure figures rise from Moonlight's soul, painfully writhing each and every one vertiginously struggling in the madness of genius, the madness of Existence, of Spirit…, and in that supreme vertigo in which torture and convulsion are madly mixed and mingled, a sinister spot of light, in a vague expression of a dream, is sketched in the background through the lividity of death as if indifferent to the dismal whirlwind of pain that only the soul of Moonlight knows how to create!… It is the artist who, spiritualized in the sublime conception of the model, in the obscure hallucination of his strange soul vaguely wandering in aesthete cynicism, coldly admires the pain that, in a prodigious struggle, the spasm of death intensifies through an infinite chaos of convulsive vertigo… Of its own dark core the soul of Moonlight tears breathless whirlwinds, but as impetuous waves completely shatter, lost against the tragic granite, the tempestuous torrents of that splendid spiritual ocean terrifyingly break through the rigid, impenetrable webs of the artist's soul!

All that gigantic convulsionism that sublimates Moonlight, that invincible, burning longing to dominate the artist through an inept debauchery, the model can no longer withstand, but falls into infinite prostration in which his whole soul dissolves, and he becomes like a nocturnal field from a past battle which a pale, somber light of the moon vaguely illuminates, the vague light which the artist with his entire soul then exhales... The artist was the vague light of the last quadrant when, in a delirium of death, in an unconscious cavalcade, tenebrous clouds enveloped it in convulsions without enrapturing it, and now, ever serene, cold, lugubrious, his pale light pours into the soul of the model through a vague silent mist of melancholy haze in which the soul of Moonlight wholly exhales itself, vanishing...!

Moonlight burns again like a torrent of fire, and from his instantaneous rest, rises suddenly, in a formidable rush upon the artist, launching himself, emboldening him with kisses in which he wants to enrapture his soul! In convulsions that rest has fed, his whole spirit sets, becomes indomitable, gigantic, impetuous as a spiteful wave raised by a volcano, a devastating torrent of Apocalyptic Fatality!...

The astonished artist looks at it, and in that impetuous rush, both crash to the ground, forgetting the dream, the hallucination... Peace returns to the spirits, a gloomy peace, full of sinister forebodings! The paroxysm of pain could not be reached, was lost for both...!

. . . .

It's been a few days. He looks at the model from a different angle, suffers a deep commotion in his spirit, almost feels his soul... He embodies himself in the dark harshness of his tragic spirit, feels it more beautiful, more profound, sublime...! The varied trances in which Moonlight had abruptly launched himself on that tragic afternoon, that variety of trances that the model had so vigorously endured, distresses his soul. He no longer only admires him, but longs for him with ardor and yearning...

He seeks him everywhere, and finally, finding him, with a lusty spirit, says to him: "I have never understood you, Moonlight, as I now understand you. Perhaps I would still not understand you if I had yielded to your desire right away. But I had time to reflect, to dream of you. Your strange nobility, which, after my astonishment, suddenly calmed your nerves, deeply impressed me, the contrasts of your soul are wonderful, only your sublime, ingenious personality... could withstand such wild swings of character! For this I want you, your longing is the same as mine today; without your deep kisses I can not go on, my flesh will be intrenched in yours so that in your soul it is wholly spiritualized!..." And he looks for his mouth. Moonlight gently pushes him away, saying, only "I have also reflected, dreamed... Tomorrow you will know my dream."

The next day, the artist receives a letter that contains the following terms:

My dear friend

You may find it strange that I only now expose you to my final dream but I need all of my soul and only when I write, does it gush torrentially in gurgles from myself. Without the quill I remain in tragic concentration, barely showing others my spirit. Because the effusion of the soul on paper is almost spiritual, the soul does not exteriorize in excess, nor materialize impurely.

Tell me, if in a drama, if in a vigorous tragedy, a formidable storm were to unleash itself in a fatal paroxysm, finally reaching, making it banal, a definite limit: would you admire such a tragedy?... The indefinite that we aspire to in art, that longing for the ideal is worth more to us than the ideal, that longing, that infinite and never satisfied desire must fill up our lives and become the highest expression of pure art!...

Existence is vertiginous and spiritual, its vertigo — transcendent! In the Pure Spirit that extension transcends, where vertigo is personalized, consubstantiated, completely accentuated, it will never know such extension. It does not spread out in a mechanical activity, it is spiritual activity, pure dynamism!... This is its beauty, its own existence which, only in this way, all confused in a Whole, in the Infinitesimal, in the Monad, is fully accentuated!... Spiritual convulsionism is sublime and only it is sublime! Whence derives its sublimity? From its energy which is only accentuated in the Spirit, in the Monad!...

There is thus, in the convulsive vertigo of Existence a dark expansion. Total activity, all the energy that forms it, doesn't expand in space and time, but remains tortured in the Infinitesimal. It is infinite, achieves everything eternally, infinitismalizing itself, spiritualizing itself thus...

It exists only in the transcendental, only there does it struggle eternally.

It has an expansion, an infinite freedom which, as infinite, reaches everything eternally, as if eternally self-destructing!... It is transcendent, if it only exists in the Transcendental, if in the same infinitesimal point, in the Monad, it struggles eternally, only to contort itself in infinite torture... And does not the pain and above all the yearning express the convulsive, tortured, contorted, transcendence of the pure spiritual act?... is this not the sublime expression of Vertigo? In pain, in yearning, we must live!

The supreme transcendentalisation of pure energy, by spiritualizing it, absolutely undefines it. The Infinitesimal in which energy eternally struggles, contains absolute indefinitism. And does the activity itself not already express the Indefinite?... When transcendent, its indefiniteness absolute, it becomes Vertigo! And what is the yearning, the yearning itself, if not the privileged threshold of this Pure Vertigo, its magnificent symptom, its human manifestation?... To the indefinite in art we aspire, to an indefinite full of torture, to a "rafiné" like that which the genius of Baudelaire understood. And when that torture of the Indefinite fills our innermost soul, then, full of yearning — as Nietzsche nearly willed it — it almost reaches the eternal paroxysm of

Existence that struggles wholly in Infinite Vertigo! And not only in art should there be longing but also in life, the painful longing for the Undefined!

Yearning is not just pain, it is not just any pain. When it is not understood, when in its supreme beauty it cannot be felt, it can be depressing, humiliating! The sharp, virilizing pain, the profound and amoral pain, the pain in which the I dominates, the pain of spirit... that is the supreme pain... the aesthetic pain! To dominate in pain, to feel the strength of living in it, endless pleasure...! And does not the transcendental torture of Existence fully express the supreme pain, the personalizing pain, in which Vertigo wholly accentuates itself, imposes itself, personalizes itself?...

Let us turn away our flesh. If we satisfied it, no, if we satisfied the spirit because it alone acts through the flesh, we would trivialize ourselves, give a bourgeois ending to our drama. It would have an end, a determined limit in which, soon, our souls would surely become over satiated. Let us be aesthetes, let us live eternal in longing since it only, personalizes the soul, making it gigantic to our spiritual view... My request is strange, but isn't the Vertigo of Existence strange?...

Adieu!...

Moonlight.

January 1913.

RAUL LEAL.

(From the unpublished book *Reveries and Hallucinations.*)

POEMS

BY AN ANONYMOUS WRITER CALLED

VIOLANTE DE CYSNEIROS

N. B. — These beautiful poems, created by an anonymous sick intelligence, appeared to us in the Editing Room. We publish them because they are worthy, caring little about the vital personalities from which they emanate. Every work of art is the justification of itself.

Orpheu.

TO ALVARO DE CAMPOS,

THE MASTER.

In the black and ancient night
There is only the Lighthouse light:
Now yellow, the color of the sun,
Now red, like an enemy.

In the deep black heart
Of the night sleeping in darkness
The Lighthouse is Another World,
Now crying, now laughing.

In the dark night, after all,
Everything is restricted:
Only the Lighthouse is real!

The darkness never ends,
O infinite sensation,
— Now I am but a Lighthouse to Myself!

June, 1915.

*

*   *

The whole of my Soul traps itself
In that form of grace;
But not in living form
But in the Line that passes.

The whole of my Soul traps itself,
Flaps its Wings — flutters…
Like the distant shadow
Of that Line that passes.

Life is only the Space
That goes from the Line itself
To its shadow in a trace.

When Death is at the door,
Merged in the same Space
It will all be the same Line.

June, 1915.

TO ALVARO DE CAMPOS,

    THE MASTER.

I

Beyond those hills
There are no birds, nor fountains,
Nor streams, nor meadows,
Nor houses by the ridge.

Beyond those hills
There are no secrets of fountains,
Nor Shadows in the Avenues,
Nor grasses, footsteps or silks.

Beyond those hills
There are no arches of bridges,
Nor delicate maiden hands,
Nor lakes, boats or sails.

II

Beyond those hills
There is only Space!
Space and time are Bridges
That God has in his lap.

Absent Bridges that connect
Infinity and Eternity.
Only sensations are Present,
Only in them lives the Truth.

The Past has never passed,
The Future, I cannot possess
Since I am always Present
In what I Was, I Am and Will Be.

June, 1915.

TO SR. MARIO DE SÁ-CARNEIRO.

Just now as as I was embroidering
I pricked my fingertips with
The needle I was using to embroider…

And the pure white silk,
White as the color of my fingers,
That silk which was white
Became stained with red poppies…

Because the blood in my veins
Has already created red poppies…

So alone and so removed!

June, 1915.

TO SR. FERNANDO PESSOA.

Nothing in Me is necessary
Not even what was dreamed,
O beads of my rosary
Of a dream never ended.

Everything is so made of Me…
Only my distant past
Is like an endless dream
That the Other dreamed.

I cross my arms. I don't speak.
I hear a pain-stricken voice
Within Me evoking it.

Sailor! Lost Island!
And my senses dreaming it
Is the truth of life.

June, 1915.

TO SR. ALFREDO PEDRO GUISADO.

Over mysteries of the past
I stood up in a curve and standing
From my body I made meaning
In a dream of Salomé.

Curved, my aching eyes…
Curved my hands and arms…
All my body is parts
From the mirrors of meanings…

I danced… I danced… And Seeing Myself
All curved and standing
Was the meaning of Being Me

Present in my gaze
I was Another Salomé
Made of Myself dancing.

June, 1915.

TO SR. CÔRTES-RODRIGUES.

I pass through the world living it,
I pass through the world feeling it,
And this color of my hair
Is seeing it and owning it.

I pass through the world dreaming it,
As a way of living it,
And my way of looking at it
Is my way of seeing it.

Only in Myself do I concretize
And the Dream of my life
In that Dream I realize it.

And always Present in Myself,
All My Being is limited
In Me Truly Being Myself.

June, 1915.

TO MYSELF

TWO YEARS AGO

My hands are slender,
They are white spindles of ermine
Where you spun and don't spin
The Dream of your affection.

My hands are slender,
My nails are pink,
And every day
I put on your ointment.

When I polish them
Your smiling mouth runs
Through them anxiously…

But my i shaped fingers
Speak of the long distance
That goes from Me to You.

June, 1915.

VIOLANTE DE CYSNEIROS.

MARITIME ODE

BY

ÁLVARO DE CAMPOS

to Santa Rita Pintor.

Maritime Ode

———

On this summer morning, alone, on the deserted pier,
Gazing towards the side of the inlet, eyeing the Undefined,
I look and it makes me happy to see,
Small, black and clear, a packet boat entering the pier.
Still far off, yet distinct, classic in its own way.
It leaves the futile brim of its smoke in the distant air behind it.
It enters, and the morning enters with it, and in the river,
Here, there, the sea life awakens,
Sails are raised, tugboats advance,
Small boats appear behind the ships in the port.
There is a vague breeze.
But my soul is with what I see least,
With the incoming ship,
With the Distance, with the Morning,
With the maritime sense of this Hour,
With the aching sweetness that rises in me like nausea,
Like one beginning to get seasick in spirit.

I look at the liner from a distance, with a great independence of soul,
And inside me a steering wheel starts to turn, slowly.

The liners that enter the inlet in the morning
Bring to my eyes
The joyful sad mystery of those who come and go.
They bring memories of distant docks and other moments
Of another mode of the same humanity in other ports
Every docking, every ship setting sail
Is — I feel it in me like my blood —
Unconsciously symbolic, terrifyingly
Threatening with metaphysical significance
And it disturbs in me who I was…

Ah, the whole pier is nostalgia in stone!
And when the ship leaves the pier
And suddenly one notices that a space has opened up
Between the pier and the ship,
A new anguish comes over me, I don't know why,
A fog of sad feelings
That shines in the sun of my grassy anguish
Like the first window hit by the dawn,
Surrounds me with the memory of another person
That had been mysteriously mine.

Ah, who knows, who knows,
If I haven't already left long ago, before myself,
From a pier; if I haven't left, on a ship in the oblique sun of dawn,
Another kind of port?
Who knows if I haven't left, before the hour
The outside world appears to
Rise for me,
A great pier full of a few people,
A great half-awakened city,
An enormous commercial city, fully grown, apoplectic,
As much as that can be outside of Space and Time?

Yes, of a pier, of a pier in some material way,
Real, visible as a pier, a veritable pier,
The Absolute Pier by whose unconsciously imitated model,
Insensibly evoked,
We men build
Our piers at our ports,
Our piers of actual stone over real water,
That after being built suddenly announce themselves
Real-Things, Spirit-Things, Entities in Stone-Souls,
At certain moments of our root-feeling
When in the outside world a door is opened
And, with nothing changing,
Everything turns out to be diverse.

Ah the Great Pier from where we left in Nation-Ships!
The Great Prior Pier, eternal and divine!
From what port? In what waters? And why do I think this?
Great Pier like the other piers, but Unique.
Like them, full of whispery silences at dawn,
And blooming with the noisy morning cranes
And freight train arrivals,
And under the light black occasional cloud
From the bottom of the chimneys of the nearby factories

Shadowing its black floor with small coal shards that shine,
As if it were the shadow of a cloud that passed over dark water.

Ah, such essentiality of mystery and meaning
Frozen in divine revealing ecstasy
Is not a bridge between any pier and The Pier
But the hour of the color of silence and anguish!

The Pier reflected blackly in the still waters,
The hustle on board the ships,
O wandering unstable soul of the people who live aboard,
Of the symbolic people who pass by and with whom nothing lasts,
For whom there is always change on board
When the ship returns to port!

O continuous escapes, departures, drunkenness of the Diverse!
Eternal soul of navigators and navigation!
Hulls reflected slowly in the waters,
When the ship leaves the port!
To float as the soul of life, to depart as a voice,
To live the moment tremulously over eternal waters.
To wake up to days more direct than European days.
To see mysterious ports on the solitude of the sea,
To turn remote capes that pass suddenly into vast landscapes
Through innumerable astonished slopes…

Ah, the distant beaches, the piers seen from afar,
And then the nearby beaches, the piers seen up close.
The mystery of each departure and arrival,
The painful instability and incomprehensibility
Of this impossible universe
More intensely felt with every maritime hour!
The absurd sobbing that our souls pour out
Over the expanse of different seas with islands in the distance,
Over the coasts of distant islands left behind,
Over the clear growth of the ports, with their houses and their people,
To the approaching ship.

Ah, the freshness of the mornings when one arrives,
And the pallor of the mornings when one departs,
When our guts crease up
With a vague sensation like fear
— The ancestral fear of moving away and departing,
The mysterious ancestral apprehension of Arrival and Newness —
Shrinks our skin and nauseates us,
And our whole distressed body feels,

As if it were our soul,
An inexplicable desire to be able to feel this in another way:
A nostalgia for something,
A disturbance of affections for which vague homeland?
For what coast? what ship? what pier?
Our thoughts sicken,
And there only remains a big void inside us,
A hollow satiety of maritime minutes,
And a vague anxiety that would be boredom or pain
If it knew how to be it...

The summer morning is still a little cool.
A light nighttime drowsiness blows in the air.
The steering wheel inside me accelerates slightly.
And the packet boat is coming in, because it must be coming in,
And not because I see it moving in its excessive distance.

In my imagination it is already close and visible
In all the length of the lines of its portholes...
And everything shakes inside me, all my flesh and skin,
Because of that creature that never arrives on any boat
And that I came to wait for at the pier today, by an oblique mandate.

The ships that enter the inlet,
The ships that leave the ports,
The ships that pass by in the distance
(I imagine seeing them from a deserted beach) —
All these ships almost abstract on their departure
All these ships move me as if they were something else
And not just ships, ships coming and going.

And the ships seen at close range, even if one is not going to board them,
Seen from below, from the dinghies, the high metal-plaited walls,
Seen inside, through the chambers, the rooms, the pantries,
Looking at the masts up close, tapering up high,
Grazing the ropes, walking down the uncomfortable stairs,
Smelling the greased metallic and maritime mix of it all —
Ships seen from close up are something else and the same thing,
They give the same longing and the same yearning in another way.

All maritime life! everything about maritime life!
All that fine seduction creeps into my blood
And I muse indeterminately about travelling.
Ah, the lines of the distant coasts, flattened by the horizon!
Ah, the capes, the islands, the sandy beaches!
Maritime loneliness as certain moments in the Pacific

In which, I don't know by what suggestion learned at school,
For being the largest of the oceans, feels heavy on the nerves
And the world and the taste of things become a desert within us!
The most human, most speckled, stretch of the Atlantic!
The Indian Ocean, the most mysterious of all oceans!
The Mediterranean, sweet, without any mystery, classic, a sea to beat
Against terraces viewed from nearby gardens by white statues!
All seas, all straits, all bays, all gulfs,
I want to squeeze them to my chest, feel them close and die!

And you, O naval things, my old dream toys!
Compose my inner life outside of me!
Keels, masts and sails, rudder wheels, cords,
Chimneys of steam, propellers, topsails, streamers,
Tiller ropes, hatches, boilers, steam pipes, valves;
I fell inside myself in heaps, in heaps,
Like the messy contents of a drawer dumped on the floor!
Be the treasure of my feverish greed,
Be the fruit of the tree of my imagination,
Subject of my songs, blood in the veins of my intelligence,
Yours be the bond that unites me to the outside by aesthetics,
Provide me with image-metaphors, literature,
Because in real truth, seriously, literally,
My sensations are a boat turned upside down,
My imagination a half-submerged anchor,
My yearning a broken oar,
And the fabric of my nerves is a net drying on the beach!

Unexpectedly, the sound of a whistle from the river, just one.
The whole floor of my psyche is already trembling.
The steering wheel inside me accelerates more and more.

Ah, the packet boats, the voyages, not knowing the whereabouts
of so-and-so, our maritime acquaintance!
Ah, the glory of knowing that a man who spent time with us
Drowned near a Pacific island!
We who spent time with him will tell everyone about it,
With legitimate pride, trusting invisibly
In that which has a more beautiful and wider meaning
Than just the boat that he was in having been lost
And he having sunken to the bottom because he got water in his lungs!

Ah, the packet boats, the coal ships, the sailing ships!
They are becoming rarer — alas! — sailing ships in the seas!
And I, who love modern civilization, I who kiss machines with my soul,
I the engineer, I the civilized, I the one who was educated abroad,

I would like to have only sailboats and wooden boats next to my sight,
To not know of other maritime life than the old life of the seas!
Because ancient seas are Absolute Distance,
Pure Distance, freed from the weight of the Present...
And ah, how everything here reminds me of that better life,
Where seas were bigger and more mysterious because people
Sailed more slowly and because less was known about them.

All the steam in the distance is a boat sailing nearby.

Any distant ship seen now is a ship in the past seen close.
All invisible sailors aboard ships on the horizon
Are the visible sailors from the time of the old ships,
From the slow season of dangerous sailing in sailboats,
From the wood and canvas era of travel that took months.

Little by little the delirium of maritime things takes over me,
The pier and its atmosphere physically penetrate me,
The swell of the Tagus climbs over my senses,
And I start to dream, I start to get involved in the dream of the waters,
In my soul, the transmission belts start to run smoothly
And the acceleration of the steering wheel clearly shakes me.

The waters call for me,
The seas call for me.
The distance calls for me, raising a corporeal voice,
The maritime epochs all felt in the past, call out to me.

You, English sailor, Jim Barns, my friend, it was you
Who taught me that ancient English cry, that,
For complex souls like mine,
So poisonously sums up
The confused call of the waters,
The unprecedented and implicit voice of all things in the sea,
Shipwrecks, distant journeys, dangerous crossings.
That English cry of yours, made universal in my blood,
Without the shape of a cry, without human form or voice,
That tremendous scream that seems to sound
From inside a cave whose dome is the sky
And seems to narrate all the sinister things
That can happen in the Distance, in the Sea, throughout the Night...
(You always pretended to call for a schooner,
And you'd say, putting a hand on each side of your mouth,
Being the spokesperson for the great hardened dark hands:

Aho-o-o-o-o-o-o-o-o-o---yyyy…
Schooner aho-o-o-o-o-o-o-o-o-o-o-o-o-o---yyyy…)

I hear you from here, now, and I wake up to something.
The wind shudders. The morning rises. The heat opens.
I feel my cheeks blush.
My conscious eyes dilate.
The ecstasy in me rises, grows and progresses,
And with a blind rowdy noise
The lively turning of the steering wheel is accentuated.

O clamorous call
To whose heat, to whose fury all my yearnings
Boil in me in an explosive unit,
My own boredom made dynamic, all of it!…
A plea directed to my blood
From a past love, I don't know where, that returns
And still has the strength to attract and pull me,
That still has the strength to make me hate this life
That I spend between the physical and psychical impenetrability
Of the real people I live with!

Ah, however it may be, to wherever it may be, to depart!
To set sail out there, over the waves, through the danger, over the sea.
To go Far, to go Abroad, into the Abstract Indefinite Distance,
Into the mysterious and deep nights,
Carried, like dust, by winds, by gales!
To go, go, go, go for good!
All my blood rages for wings!
My whole body is thrown forward!
I leap through my imagination in torrents!
I run over myself, I roar, I rush!…
My yearnings burst in foam
And my flesh is a wave hitting rocks!

Thinking about this — O rage! thinking about this — O fury!
Thinking about this narrowness of my life full of yearnings,
Suddenly, tremulously, extraorbitantly,
With a vicious, vast, violent oscillation,
Of the living wheel of my imagination,
The gloomy and sadistic heat of the strident maritime life,
Breaks through me, whistling, hissing, dizzying.

Hey sailors, topmen! hey crew, pilots!
Navigators, seamen, sailors, adventurers!

Hey captains of ships! men at the helm and on masts!
Men who sleep on coarse bunks!
Men who sleep with Danger peeking through the portholes!
Men who sleep with Death as a pillow!
Men on quarterdecks, on bridges from where to gaze at
The immense immensity of the immense sea!
Hey manipulators of cargo cranes!
Hey abaters of sails, stokers, stewards!
Men who put the cargo in the cellars!
Men who roll up cables on the deck!
Men who clean the metal from the hatches!
Helm men! machine men! mast men!
Hey-ey-ey-ey-ey-ey-ey!
People with caps! People with knitted sweaters!
People with crossed anchors and flags embroidered on their chest!
Tattooed people! people with pipes! railing people!
People with dark skins from getting so much sun, parched from so much rain,
With their eyes clean from so much immensity before them,
With a bold face from so many winds that truly hit them!
Hey-ey-ey-ey-ey-ey-ey!
Men who have seen Patagonia!
Men who passed through Australia!
Who filled their gaze with coasts that I will never see!
Who landed on lands where I will never go ashore!
Who bought crude items in colonies on the prow of the backwoods!
And you did it all like it was nothing!
As if that were natural,
As if life were that,
Like not even fulfilling a destiny!
Hey-ey-ey-ey-ey-ey-ey!
Men of the current sea! men of the past sea!
Stewards! galley slaves! fighters of Lepanto!
Pirates of the time of Rome! Greek navigators!
Phoenicians! Carthaginians! Portuguese flung from Sagres
To the indefinite adventure, to the Absolute Sea, to accomplish the Impossible!

Hey-ey-ey-ey-ey-ey-ey-ey-ey!
Men who erected stone monuments, who gave names to capes!
Men who negotiated with blacks for the first time!
Who first sold slaves from new lands!
Who gave the first European spasm to astonished black women!
Who brought gold, beads, fragrant woods, arrows,
From slopes exploding in green vegetation!
Men who plundered tranquil African villages,
Who made these races flee with the sound of cannons,
Who killed, stole, tortured, won

Novelty prizes like those who, with their heads down
Hurl themselves against the mystery of new seas! Hey-ey-ey-ey-ey!
To you all in one, to all of you in all of you as one,
To you all mixed, intertwined,
To you all bloody, violent, hated, feared, sacred,
I salute you, I salute you, I salute you!
Hey-ey-ey-ey ey! Hey ey-ey-ey ey! Hey-ey-ey ey-ey-ey ey!
Hey laho-laho-laHO-laha-a-a-a-a!

I want to go with you, I want to go with you,
With all of you at the same time
Everywhere you went!
I want to meet your dangers face to face,
Feel in my face the winds that have wrinkled yours.
Spit out the salt of the seas that your lips kissed,
Labor in your work, share your storms,
Finally, reach extraordinary ports like you!
Escape civilization with you!
Lose the notion of morals with you!
Feel my humanity change in the distance!
Drink with you in southern seas
New savagery, new bedlam of the soul,
New central fires in my volcanic spirit!
Go with you, undress — ah! get out of here! —
My civilized attire, my mildness of action,
My innate fear of chains,
My peaceful life,
My sedentary, static, ruled and revised life!

At sea, at sea, at sea, at sea,
Hey! to put my life in the sea, in the wind,
In waves!
To season with the salt of foam thrown by the winds
My taste for great travels.
To flog the flesh of my adventure with whipping water,
To penetrate the bones of my existence with oceanic cold,
To flagellate, cut, wrinkle with winds, foams, suns,
My cyclonic and Atlantic being,
My nerves displayed like rigging,
A lyre at the hands of the winds!

Yes, yes, yes... Crucify me in navigation
And my shoulders will enjoy my cross!
Bind me to travels as if to stakes
And the sensation of the stakes will enter my spine
And I will start to feel them in a vast passive spasm!

Do what you want with me, as long as it is in the seas,
On decks, to the sound of waves,
Tear me apart, kill me, bruise me!
What I want is to take unto Death
A soul overflowing with Sea,
Drunk and collapsing from maritime things,
From sailors and anchors, from cables,
From the distant coasts and the noise of the winds
From the Expanse and the Pier, from shipwrecks
And the quiet shops,
From the masts and the waves,
Voluptuously taking unto Death with pain,
A body full of leeches, sucking, sucking,
Strange green absurd sea leeches!

Make rigging of my veins!
Moorings of my muscles!
Pull my skin off, pin it to the keels.
And may I feel and never stop feeling the pain of the nails!
Make an admiral's pennant of my heart
In the hour of war of the old ships!
Trample my pulled out eyes on the decks!
Break my bones against the boat rails!
Flog me tied to the masts, flog me!
To all the winds of all latitudes and longitudes
Spill my blood over the hurled waters
That cross the ship, the quarterdeck, from one side to the other,
In the angry convulsion of the storms!

To have the audacity of the wind through the sailcloths!
To be like the tall crow's nests, the whistle of the winds!
The old Fado guitar of the seas full of dangers,
Songs for the navigators to hear and not repeat!

The sailors who rose up
They hung the captain on lintel.
They landed another on a desert island.
Marooned!
The tropical sun put the fever of ancient piracy
In my intensive veins.
The Patagonian winds tattooed my imagination
With tragic and obscene images.
Fire, fire, fire, inside me!
Blood! blood! blood! blood!
My whole brain explodes!
The world breaks for me in red!

SANTA RITA PINTOR. — Geometrical synthesis of a head × infinite plastic environment ×
PARIS YEAR 1913.   physical transcendentalism

(RADIOGRAPHIC SENSITIVITY.)

My veins burst with the sound of moorings!
The song of the Great Pirate snaps inside me,
Fierce, voracious,
The yelling death of the Great Pirate singing
Until he slid terror down his men's spines.
There from the stern of the ship, dying and yelling, singing:

> *Fifteen men on the Dead Man's Chest.*
> *Yo-ho ho and a bottle of rum!*

And then screaming, in an already unreal voice, bursting into the air:

Darby M'Graw-aw-aw-aw-aw!
Darby M'Graw-aw-aw-aw-aw-aw-aw-aw!
Fetch a-a-aft the ru-u-u-u-u-u-u-u-um, Darby.

Hiyah, what a life! that was the life, hiyah!
Hey-ey-ey-ey-ey-ey-ey!
Hey-laho-laho!-LaHO-laha-ha-la-a-a!
Hey-ey-ey-ey-ey-ey-ey!

Broken keels, ships to the bottom, blood in the seas!
Decks full of blood, body fragments!
Fingers severed over the rails!
Children's heads, here, there!
People with their eyes out, screaming, howling!
Hey-ey-ey-ey-ey-ey-ey-ey-ey-ey!
Hey-ey-ey-ey-ey-ey-ey-ey-ey-ey!
I wrap myself in all this like a cape in the cold!
I rub myself against all this like a cat in heat against a wall!
I roar like a hungry lion at all this!
I charge like a crazy bull against all this!
I dig in my nails, I break my claws; I bleed from the teeth over this!
Hey-ey-ey-ey-ey-ey-ey-ey-ey-ey!

Suddenly the old scream cracks next to my ears,
Like a bugle at my side,
But now angry, metallic,
Calling out the prey on sight,
The schooner that is to be taken:

Aho-o o-o-o-o-o-o-o-o---yyyy…
Schooner aho-o-o-o-o-o-o-o-o-o---yyyy…

The whole world doesn't exist for me! I burn red!
I roar in the fury of the approach!

Chief Pirate! Caesar-Pirate!
I plunder, I kill, I shatter, I tear!
I only feel the sea, the prey, the loot!
I only feel the beating, my veins beating in my temples
My sensation oozes hot blood from my eyes!
Hey-ey-ey-ey-ey-ey-ey-ey-ey-ey!

Ah pirates, pirates, pirates!
Pirates, love me and hate me!
Mix me with you, pirates!

Your fury, your cruelty, speak to the blood
In a woman's body that once was mine and whose heat survives!

I wanted to be an animal representative of all your gestures,
An animal that sank its teeth into the rails, into the keels,
That ate masts, drank blood and tar on decks,
Bit sails, oars, rigging and pulley blocks,
Female and monstrous sea serpent fattening up in crimes!

And there is a symphony of incompatible and analogous sensations.
There is an orchestration in my blood of a bedlam of crimes,
Of spasmodic clashes of blood orgies in the seas,
Ragingly, like a gale of heat in the spirit,
Hot dust cloud clouding my lucidity
And making me see and dream it all with only my skin and veins!

The Pirates, piracy, boats, the hour,
That sea hour when prey is assaulted,
And the terror of the captives escapes to madness — that hour,
In its totality of crimes, terror, boats, people, sea, sky, clouds,
Voicing the breeze, latitude, longitude,
I wanted it to be Fully in my body as a Whole, suffering,
To be my body and my blood, to compose my being in red,
To bloom like a wound itching in the unreal flesh of my soul!

Ah, to be everything in crime! to be all component elements
Of boat raids and massacres and rape!
To be whatever was where looting happened!
To be whatever lived or laid at the site of blood tragedies!
To be the pirate-summary of all piracy at its height,
And the victim-synthesis, in flesh and blood, of all the pirates of the world!

Being, in my passive body, the all-women-woman
Who were raped, killed, injured, torn by the pirates!
To be in my subjugated being the female that has to be theirs

And to feel it all — all these things at once — down my spine!

O my hairy and rude heroes of adventure and crime!
My seafaring beasts, husbands of my imagination!
Casual lovers of the obliquity of my sensations!
I wanted to be the One who waited for you at the ports,
You, hated loved ones of pirate blood in dreams!
Because she would have, but only in spirit, raged with you
Over the naked corpses of the victims you make at sea!
Because she would have accompanied your crime, and in the oceanic orgy
Her sibylline spirit would dance invisibly around the gestures
Of your bodies, of your cleavers, of your strangling hands!
And she on land, waiting for you, when you came, if you came,
Would drink in the roars of your love all the vast,
Foggy and sinister perfume of your victories,
And hiss a red and yellow sabbath through spasms!

The torn flesh, the flesh open and gutted, the blood running!
Now, at the concise height of dreaming what you did
I completely lose myself, I no longer belong to you, I am you,
My femininity that accompanies you is to be your souls!
To be inside of all your ferocity, when you practiced it!
Suck the inside of your awareness of your sensations
When you dyed the high seas with blood,
When you occasionally threw to sharks
The still living bodies of the wounded, the pink flesh of the children
And took the mothers to the rails to see what happened to them!

To be with you in the carnage, in the plunder!
To be orchestrated with you in the symphony of looting!
Ah, I don't know what, I don't know how much of you I wanted to be!
Not just being your female, being your females, being your victims,
Being your victims — men, women, children, ships —,

Not just the time and the boats and the waves,
Not just being your souls, your bodies, your fury, your possession,
Not just being your abstract act of orgy concretely,
It wasn't just this that I wanted to be — it was more than this, the God-this!
It was necessary to be God, the God of an inside out cult,
A monstrous and satanic God, a God of a pantheism of blood,
In order to fill the whole measure of my imaginative fury,
So I could never exhaust my desires for identity
With each and everything, and the more-than-everything of your victories!

Ah, torture me to heal me!
My flesh — make it the air that your knives cut through

Before they fall on heads and shoulders!
My veins be the garments that your knives transpierce!
My imagination the body of women you rape!
My intelligence the deck where you are standing killing!
My whole life, in its nervous, hysterical, absurd ensemble,
The great organism from which every act of piracy that was committed
Was a conscious cell — and all of me swirled
Like an immense rippling rot, and was all of that!

With such unreasonable, dreadful speed,
The feverish machine of my overflowing visions
Gyrates now that my volant conscience,
Is but a foggy circle whistling through the air.

> *Fifteen men on the Dead Man's Chest*
> *Yo-ho ho and a bottle of rum!*

Hey-laho-laho-laHO----laha-a-aaa---aaa...

Ah! the savagery of this savagery! Fuck
Every life like ours, which is nothing like this!
I, turned engineer, practical by force, sensitive to everything
Here, stationary, in relation to you, even when I walk;
Even when I act, inert; even when I impose myself, feeble;
Static, broken, cowardly dissident of your Glory,
Of your great shrill, hot and bloody dynamic!

Damn! for not being able to act according to my delirium!
Damn! for always clinging to the skirts of civilization!
For walking with the *douceur des moeurs* on my back, like a bundle of lace!

Corner boys — of modern humanitarianism — all of us!
Stupored hectics, neurasthenics, lymphatics,
Without the courage to be violent and audacious people,
With the soul of a chicken caught by a leg!

Ah, the pirates! the pirates!
The yearning for the illegal united with the fierce,
The craving for absolutely cruel and abominable things
That gnaw at our thin bodies in abstract heat,
Our feminine and delicate nerves,
The big crazy fevers in our empty eyes!

Force me to kneel before you!
Humble me and beat me!
Make me your slave and your thing!

And may your contempt for me never leave me,
O my lords! O my lords!

To always gloriously take the submissive part
In bloody events and stretched sensualities!
Crumble over me, like great heavy walls,
O barbarians of the ancient sea!
Tear me up and hurt me!
From the east to the west of my body
Streak my flesh with blood!
Kiss with nautical knives and lashes and anger
My joyous carnal terror of belonging to you.
My masochistic urge to give myself to your fury,
To be the inert and sentient object of your omnivorous cruelty,
Dominators, lords, emperors, steeds!
Ah, torture me,
Rip me open!
Break me into conscious pieces
Spill me out on the decks,
Spread me out in the seas, leave me
On the avid beaches of the islands!

Satiate yourselves over me with all my mysticism about you!
Carve my soul with blood
Cut, scratch!
O tattoo artists of my corporeal imagination!
Beloved skinners of my carnal submission!
Subjugate me like one who kills a dog with kicks!
Make me the well for your contempt of dominion!

Make me all your victims!
As Christ suffered for all men, I want to suffer
For all your victims at your hands,
Your calloused, bloody hands with fingers severed
In the sudden attacks of railings!

Make something of me as if I was being
Dragged — O pleasure, O kissed pain! —
Dragged by the tail of horses whipped by you...
But this in the sea, this in se-a-a-a, this in the SE-A-A-A!
Hey-ey-ey-ey-ey! Hey-ey-ey-ey-ey-ey-ey! EY-EY-EY-EY-EY-EY!
                                                    In SE-E-E-A!
Yeh eh-eh-eh-eh-eh! Yeh-eh-eh-eh-eh-eh! Yeh-eh-eh-eh-eh-eh-eh!
Everything shouts! everything screaming! winds, waves, boats,
Tides, topsails, pirates, my soul, the blood, and the air, and the air!
Eh-eh-eh-eh! Yeh-eh-eh-eh-eh! Yeh-eh-eh-eh-eh-eh! Everything sings screaming!

FIFTEEN MEN ON THE DEAD MAN'S CHEST.
YO-HO-HO AND A BOTTLE OF RUM!

Eh-eh-eh-eh-eh-eh-eh! Eh-eh-eh-eh-eh-eh-eh! Eh-eh-eh-eh-eh-eh-eh!
Eh-laho-laho-laHO-O-O-oo-laha-a-a---aaa!

AHO-O-O O O O-O-O-O O-O---yyy!…
SCHOONER AHO-O-O-O-O-O-O-O-O-O----yyyy!…

Darby M'Graw-aw-aw-aw-aw-aw!
DARBY M'GRAW-AW-AW-AW-AW-AW-AW!
FETCH A-A-AFT THE RU-U-U-U-U-UM, DARBY!

Eh-eh-eh-eh-eh-eh-eh-eh-eh-eh eh-eh-eh!
EH-EH EH-EH-EH EH-EH EH-EH EH-EH-EH!
EH-EH-EH-EH-EH-EH-EH-EH-EH EH EH-EH!
EH-EH-EH-EH-EH-EH-EH-EH-EH-EH-EH-EH!

EH-EH-EH-EH-EH-EH-EH-EH-EH-EH-EH!

Something broke in me. The red grew dark.
I felt too much to be able to continue feeling.
My soul ran out, only an echo remained inside me.
The speed of the steering wheel decreases significantly.
My dreams take their hands off my eyes a little.
Within me there is only one vacuum, a desert, a night sea.
And as soon as I feel that there is a night sea inside me,
The vast age-old cry ascends from its distances,
Is born out of its silence, again and again.
Suddenly, like a flash of sound, which makes no noise but rather tenderness,
Suddenly embracing the entire maritime horizon
Humid and gloomy human night swell,
Voice of a distant mermaid crying, calling,
It comes from the bottom of the Far, from the bottom of the Sea, from the
                                        soul of the Abysses,
And on the surface of it, like seaweed, my broken dreams float…

Aho-o-o-o-o-o-o-o-o-o---yy…
Schooner aho-o-o-o-o-o-o-o-o-o-o-o----yy…..

Ah, the dew over my excitement!
The night coolness of my inner ocean!
Behold all of me suddenly before a night at sea
Full of the enormous utterly human mystery of the night waves.
The moon rises on the horizon
And my happy childhood wakes up inside me like a tear.

My past resurfaces, as if that maritime scream
Were an aroma, a voice, the echo of a song
That called to my past
For that happiness that I will never have again.

It was in the old quiet house by the river...
(The windows in my room, and those in the dining room too,
They looked out over low houses to the nearby river,
To the Tagus, this same Tagus, but elsewhere, further down...
If I reached the same windows now, I wouldn't reach the same windows.
That time passed like the smoke of a steamboat in the open sea...)

An inexplicable tenderness,
A moved and tearful remorse,
For all those victims — especially the children —
That I made dreaming, while dreaming of being an ancient pirate,
Stirred emotion, because they were my victims;
Tender and soft, because they really weren't my victims;
A confused tenderness, like fogged glass, bluish,
Sings old songs in my poor aching soul.

Ah, how could I think, dream those things?
How far I am from what I was a few moments ago!
Hysteria of sensations — now these, now the opposite!
In the blond morning that rises, as my ear only chooses
Things according to this emotion — the swelling of the waters,
The light swell of the river waters against the piers...,
The sail passing near the other side of the river,
The distant hills, of Japanese blue,
The houses of Almada,
And what there is of softness and childhood in the morning hour!...

A seagull passing by,
And my tenderness increases.

But all this time I haven't noticed anything.
All this was just a feeling on the skin, like a caress.
All this time I never took my eyes off my distant dream,
Off my house by the river,
Off my childhood by the river,
Off my bedroom windows overlooking the river at night,
And the peace of the sparse moonlight in the waters!...
My old aunt, who loved me because of the son she lost...,
My old aunt used to put me to sleep by singing to me
(Although I was already too old for that)...
I remember and the tears fall on my heart and wash it away from life,

And a light sea breeze rises within me.
Sometimes she sang "Ship Catrinêta":

> *There goes the Ship Catrinêta*
> *Over the waters of the sea…*

Other times, in a very nostalgic and medieval melody,
It was the "Fair Princess"… I remember, and the poor old voice rises inside me
And it reminds me that I hardly remembered her afterwards, and she loved
me so much!
How ungrateful I was to her — and what did I do with my life after all?
It was the "Fair Princess"… I closed my eyes and she sang:

> *Being the Fair Princess*
> *Seated in her garden…*

I would open my eyes a little and see the window full of moonlight
And then I closed my eyes again, and in all of this I was happy.

> *Being the Fair Princess*
> *Seated in her garden,*
> *Her gold comb in her hand,*
> *She combed her hair…*

O my childhood's past, my doll that somebody broke!

Not being able to travel to the past, to that house and that affection,
I remain there always, always a child and always happy!

But all of this was the Past, a lantern on an old street corner.
Thinking this makes one cold, makes one hungry for something one can't get.
I feel some absurd remorse thinking about this.
Oh slow whirlwind of mismatched sensations!
Faint vertigo of confused things in the soul!
Broken furies, tenderness like spools of thread that children play with,
Great collapses of imagination over the eyes of the senses,
Tears, useless tears,
Light breezes of contradiction brushing the face of the soul…

I evoke, through a voluntary effort, to get out of this emotion,
I evoke, with a desperate, dry, null effort,
The Great Pirate's song, as he was dying:

> *Fifteen men on the Dead Man's Chest.*
> *Yo-ho-ho and a bottle of rum!*

But the song is a straight line badly drawn inside me…

I struggle and manage to call again before the eyes in my soul,
Again, but through an almost literary imagination,
The fury of piracy, slaughter, the appetite, almost the taste, of looting,
Of the useless slaughter of women and children,
Of futile torture, and just to distract ourselves, of poor passengers
And the sensuality of ruining and breaking the most cherished things of others,
But I dream all this with a fear of something breathing down the back of my neck.

I remember that it would be interesting
To hang children in the sight of their mothers
(But I unintentionally feel like I am their mothers),
Bury four-year-olds alive on desert islands
Taking their parents there on boats to watch
(But I shudder, remembering a son I don't have that is sleeping peacefully at home).

I'm stung with a cold craving for maritime crimes,
For an inquisition without the excuse of Faith,
Crimes not even for the reason of malice and fury,
In cold blood, not even to hurt, not even to harm,
Not even for our own fun, but just to pass the time,
Like someone who plays card games alone at a provincial dining table with
                                    the towel thrown across the table after dinner,
Just for the soft taste of committing abominable crimes and not finding them
                                    terribly exciting,
To see suffering to the point of madness and death-by-pain but never quite
                                    letting it get there…
But my imagination refuses to keep up with me.
A chill shivers me.
And suddenly, more suddenly than the other time, from farther away, from
                                    deeper down,
Suddenly — oh dread through all my veins! —,
Oh sudden cold from the door to the Mystery that opened inside me and
                                    let in a draft!
I remember God, the Transcendental part of life, and suddenly
The old voice of the English sailor Jim Barns with whom I used to speak,
Makes a voice from the mysterious tenderness within me, from the little things
                                    about my mother's lap and sister's hair ribbon,
But stupendously emanating from beyond the appearance of things,
The deaf and remote Voice becomes The Absolute Voice, The Voice Without Mouth,
Coming from above and within the night solitude of the seas,
Calling for me, calling for me, calling for me…

It comes quietly, as if it were suppressed but heard,

Far away, as if it were sounding elsewhere and could not be heard here,
Like a muffled sob, a light that goes out, a silent breath,
Nowhere in space, nowhere in time,
The eternal and nocturnal scream, the deep and confused breath:

Aho-o-o-o-o-o-o-o-o-o-o – yyy......
Aho-o-o-o-o-o-o-o-o-o-o-o-o-o – – yyy......
Schooner aho-o-o-o-o-o-o-o-o-o-o-o-o-o-o-o – – – yy.........

I shiver with the cold soul pervading my body
And suddenly open my eyes, which I hadn't closed.
Ah, what a joy to come out of dreams once and for all!
Here again is the real world, so kind on the nerves!
Here it is at this early morning hour when the packet boats that arrive early
                                                                come in.

I no longer care about the incoming packet boat. It is still far away.
Only the one which is near now washes my soul.
My hygienic, strong, practical imagination,
Is now concerned only with modern and useful things,
With cargo ships, and packet boats and passengers,
With strong, immediate, modern, commercial, true things.
The steering wheel slows down its spin inside me.

Wonderful modern sea life,
All cleanness, machinery and health!
Everything so well arranged, so spontaneously adjusted,
Every machine part, all the ships across the seas,
All the elements of the export and import commercial activity
So wonderfully combined
That everything runs as if by natural laws,
Nothing bumping into anything else!

Nothing loses its poetry. And now there are machines too
With their poetry, and all the new kinds of life
Commercial, mundane, intellectual, sentimental,
That the era of machines brought for the souls.
To travel is now as beautiful as it was before
And a ship will always be beautiful, just because it is a ship.
Traveling is still traveling and the distance is always where it has been —
Nowhere, thank God!

Ports full of steamboats of myriad species!
Small, large, of various colors, with various arrangements of portholes
From so many delightful shipping companies!

Steamboats in the ports, so individual in the detached separation of their anchorages!
So pleasurable is the quiet elegance of commercial things that sail in the sea,
In the old ever Homeric sea, O Ulysses!

O humanitarian look of the lighthouses in the distant night,
And the sudden nearby lighthouse in the very dark night
("How close to the land we were passing by!" And the sound of the water
                                                    sings to our ears)!...

All of this today is as it has always been, but there is trade;
And the commercial fate of the great steamboats makes me proud of my time!
The mix of people on board passenger ships
Gives me the modern pride of living in a time when it is so easy
For the races to mix, crossing spaces, seeing all things easily,
Enjoying life fulfilling countless dreams.

Clean, regular, modern, like an office with booths in yellow wire nets,
My feelings now, natural and measured like gentlemen,
Are practical, far from craziness, filling the lungs with sea air,
Like people perfectly aware of how hygienic it is to breathe the air of the sea.

And now time is perfectly comprised of working hours.
Everything starts to move, to regulate.

With a great natural and direct pleasure I course with my soul through
All commercial operations necessary for the shipment of goods.

My time is the stamp that all invoices carry,
And I feel that all the letters from all the offices
Should be addressed to me.

An onboard knowledge has so much individuality,
And a ship captain's signature is so beautiful and modern!
Commercial rigor of the beginning and end of letters:
Dear Sirs — Messieurs — Friends and Senhores,
Yours faithfully — ...nos salutations empressées...
All of this is not only human and clean, but also beautiful,
And at the end it has a maritime destination, a steamboat where
These goods that the letters and invoices address arrive at.

Complexity of life! Invoices are made by people
Who have loves, hates, political passions, sometimes crimes —
And they are so well written, so aligned, so independent of all that!
Some people look at an invoice and don't feel this.
Surely you, Cesário Verde, felt it.

I feel it most humanly until I tear up.
Come tell me that there is no poetry in commerce, in offices!
Rather, it enters through every pore… In this sea air I breathe it,
Because all of this is about steamboats, modern navigation,
Because invoices and business letters are the beginning of history
And the ships that carry the goods through the eternal sea are the end.

Ah, and the travels, the recreational travels, and the others,
Sea travels, where we are all companions of others
In a special way, as if a maritime mystery
Brought our souls closer and made us, for a moment,
Transitory patriots of the same uncertain homeland,
Eternally moving over the immensity of the waters
Great hotels of the Infinite, oh my cruise ships!
With the perfect and total cosmopolitanism of never stopping at one point
And containing all kinds of costumes, faces, races!

The travels, the travelers — so many species of them!
So much nationality over the world! so many careers! so many people!
So many different fates that can be given to life,
And life, after all, deep down always, always the same!
So many curious faces! All faces are curious
And nothing brings as much religiosity as looking at people a lot.
Fraternity is not, after all, a revolutionary idea.
It's something we learn through life, where we have to tolerate everything,
And end up finding what we have to tolerate amusing,
And end up crying with tenderness over what we tolerated!

Ah, all of this is beautiful, all of this is human and connected
To human feelings, so coexistent and bourgeois,
So complicatedly simple, so metaphysically sad!
Floating, diverse life ends up educating us in humanity.
Poor people! poor people all people!

I say goodbye to this hour on the body of this other ship
That is now leaving. It's an English tramp-steamer,
Very dirty, as if it was a French ship,
With the friendly air of a proletarian of the seas,
And without a doubt announced yesterday on the last page of the gazettes.

The poor steamboat warms me, it is so humble and so natural.
It seems to have a certain scruple I don't know what about, to be an honest person,
Compliant with a kind of responsibility.
There it goes, leaving the place in front of the pier where I am.
There it goes peacefully, passing by where the old ships once were

Once, once...
To Cardiff? To Liverpool? To London? It doesn't matter.
It does its duty. So let us do ours. Beautiful life!
Bon voyage! Bon voyage!
Bon voyage, my poor casual friend, who did me the favor
Of taking the fever and sadness of my dreams with you,
And restore me to life to look at you and see you pass.
Bon voyage! Bon voyage! This is life...
Such natural grooming, so inevitably morning-like
On your way out of the Lisbon harbor, today!
I have a curious and grateful affection for you because of it...
Because of what? I don't know what!... It goes... It passes...
With a slight shiver,
(T-t--t--- t---- t----- t...)
The steering wheel inside me stops.

Pass, slow steamboat, pass and don't stay...
Pass from me, pass my sight,
Get out from inside my heart.
Get lost in the Distance, in the Distant haze of God,
Get lost, follow your destiny and leave me...
Who am I to cry and interrogate?
Who am I to speak to you and love you?
Who am I that it disturbs me to see you?
Set sail off the pier, the sun rises, it rises in gold,
The roofs of the pier buildings shine,
All of this side of the city shines...
Leave, leave me, become
The first ship in the middle of the river, highlighted and clear,
Then the ship headed for the inlet, small and black,
Then a vague spot on the horizon (O my distress!),
An increasingly vague spot on the horizon...,
Afterwards, nothing, only me and my sadness,
And the big city now full of sun
And the real and naked hour, as a pier without ships,
And the slow turning of the crane that, like a rotating compass,
Draws a semicircle of I don't know what emotion
In the moved silence of my soul...

ALVARO DE CAMPOS,
Engineer.

Luís de Montalvôr

NARCISSUS

A POEM

to Fernando Pessôa.

NARCISSUS

————

The shadows of these nymphs wander through the golden afternoon!

How long will the scent of their gestures
attempt to trap my dismal eyes,
dreaming of a fatal splendor of stones?

Afternoon of temptation! What strange melodies
Disturb the sky with an ignored rumor?
Seringe! Your flute turns this deranged
afternoon that the legend recalls into enchanted rose
and blood of Illusion; and from the immortal essence
of dream this ancient hour exhumes the old idyll.

There are festive and dreamy hands in my deserted exile!

O nymphs! Beauty is for me the secret
with which God robed me in loveliness!... Oh, how I fear
dying the way I am at the hands of that desire
for the nymphs; but there is a shadow that I do not see
after and before me, and, if I sink my gaze in the eagerness
of seeing myself, I only see myself in the lap of Distance!
Let the sky sleep a little in my eyes
I do not want to open them lest I close them — God! —

Nymphs! You comb the terror at the window
of my soul through the dark and lovely hour.
I will not be crowned with defoliating flowers
but instead with white arms of loves
that open by night in a country without day...

You are the dream of me in the lap of Joy!
Your presence puts fear into my destiny.

The bowls that you pour from the sibylline aroma
of seduction, fill what you gave me with boredom,
O God!
     My being freezes to the terrestrial smile
of the virgins, which reflects the afternoon scented with
the odor of Pan!
      …And my gaze aches for I did not hide it
from the sky; since for every sleeping soul of beauty,
seraphic blue is like a nightmare!

But how to escape the dream that makes me
Foreign to myself; of a stunning blue, voracious
sad mouth, without color or human pain —
as if it were from a dream, sculpted in the hour,
triumphal and with pale flowers of the night?

Captive in myself I am like the dragon that, inviolable,
drinks the scintillation of the sonorous clarity
of sinister hair, where light burns and invades
with metalic spur the niche where it shelters…

Your hair! O it rains like gold in the night!
like threads of horror from the web of mystery…

The sterile gold splendor of your hair is aerial
like an arachnidian dream or a sidereal ceiling
chiseled into the eye — an insect's reflection —
in cold flight, in an air of sleep and gold and mourning…

Avalanches of boredom that I hear in her hair!…

  ………………………………………………………………………
  ………………………………………………………………………

I stare at the spectral flesh, as if I was before an inert frieze
of shadows, the nakedness, a line forgotten in laughter
over flames, cruel, — Jewel of chills! —
A horror of onyx snows between my cold fingers!

I contemplate my inner destiny.
      Adieu Nymphs!
My unreal gestures contain centuries of God!
In the landscape of being runs an endless river
My movements are like the other shore of me…
Soul falls in the garden of my fatal dreams.

SANTA RITA PINTOR. — Dynamic decomposition of a table + movement style
PARIS YEAR 1912.

(PLASTIC INTERSECTIONISM.)

It is always night there in the depths of my movements
where God lurks: there is moonlight in my hands
Hands shake our vain movements in the air,
— worlds of somnolence burning in reliquaries
celestial jewels, you, my solitary movements!

The sky wanders through me. And a diadem
dies on my sad and pensive brow, an emblem
of a pale soul like an old canopy or gold...
But what torpor leans me up against the vortex
like a sphinx that inclines towards an abyss and leans
over checking the soul, sister of a dream that sobs?
There is an unnamed movement awakening in my soul,
I am the rarest idea in the Garden of God!

My movements move like this water, always running
into the mouth of nothing; I lean my soul, trembling,
towards the voice of the water — sonorous crystal of alienation! —

My anxiety entangling me in the yarn of myself.

Oh ever sad water travelling through that part
of the earth that is livid like a soul fed up
with dreams! Might my absent shadow be an
air of yours — or am I the image in the current?

Whoever descended on the mystery and saw the similitude
in that intimate torpor of things, where that flight
of time in reflected shadow wearies...
I will never have two sibling gestures in life,
and if I looked back, I would be afraid of myself...
(Inter-lunar self-reflection in the dream of beyond-end...)

The one who reflects me will steal my secret.
Time drips down on us like someone in fear
Over a wall... I create eyes of being distant...
I shall put my hands on my soul as if through a quadrant...
Hands are time... and everything is a dream of itself...

I look at myself, am I not the shadow where I saw myself?...

O mirror without hour! O lustral sleep-water,
— horizontal mirror of tedium like a canal
without bottom or end. My profile is its pain!
I only reflect myself but I do not see myself in the torpor

of the water that shakes time… oh, time is the voice
that wakes up fear — sculpture of us
in the distance…
                    In rumor, in the water, I wander dementedly
and sleep with Beauty on the lap of Appearances,
that runs away like this water and this passing time
Swash of myself in the depths of my being…
Only the hands know how to have an air of continuous dreaming…

O! If the gaze falls in my hands, destinies are sketched
like arabesques…
                    I open my arms, but in vain,
and I rise from myself in the garments of commotion!

It remains for me to contemplate through the night that I flood
With myself, hanging over the appearance of the world.
My exiled shadow that I carve out in sweetness!

I disturb myself with God in the arms of Tenderness!

I feel that my voice has already crossed God!…
I grow over myself, O night of delirium!
                                    Farewell!
The image of being beautiful at the hands of my childhood.

I am the echo of a rumor broken in the distance.

Soul of the ancient night ignited with adornments!

                                    Luís de Montalvôr.

OBLIQUE RAIN

INTERSECTIONIST POEMS

BY

FERNANDO PESSOA

Oblique Rain

I

My dream of an infinite harbor crosses this landscape
From the sails of great ships, that set sail from the piers
The transparent color of the flowers, dragging in the waters in the shade,
The figures in the sun of those ancient trees…

The harbour I dream of is gloomy and pallid
And the landscape is full of sunshine on this side…
But in my spirit the sun of this day is a sombre port
And the ships leaving the harbour are these trees in the sun…

Freed in duplicity, I abandoned myself to the landscape below…
The shape of the pier is the clear and calm road
That raises itself up like a wall,
And the ships pass through the inside of the tree trunks
With a vertical horizontality,
And they let moorings fall in the water through the inside of the leaves,
                                                        one at a time…

I don't know who I dream of as myself…
Suddenly all the sea water in the port is transparent
And I look and discover at the bottom, like an enormous print,

This whole landscape, rows of trees, the burning road,
And the shadow of a ship older than the port that passes
Between my dream of the harbor and my seeing this landscape
Comes close to me, and enters inside me,
And passes to the other side of my soul…

II

The church is lit up inside the rain of this day,
And each burning candle is more rain beating against the window…

I am glad to hear the rain because it is the temple being lit,
And the windowpanes of the church seen from outside are the sound of
                                                rain heard from the inside…

The splendor of the main altar is that I'm almost unable to see the mountains
Through the rain that is such solemn gold on the altar cloth…
The Latin sounds of choral singing shakes my window pane in the wind
The feeling of having a chorus makes the water sizzle…

Mass is a car that passes
Through the faithful who kneel down on today being a sad day…
Sudden wind shakes in greater splendor
The festivity of the cathedral and the noise of rain absorbs everything
Until one only hears the voice of the water priest getting lost in the distance
With the sound of car wheels…

And the lights of the church go out
In the rain that ceases…

III

The Great Sphynx of Egypt dreams into this paper…
I write — and it appears to me through my transparent hand
And at the corner of the paper the pyramids rise…

I write — and it disturbs me to see the mouth of my quill
Become the profile of King Cheops…
Suddenly I stop…
Everything goes dark… I fall into an abyss made of time…
I am buried under the pyramids writing verses in the clear light of this lamp
And all of Egypt crushes me from above through the traces I make with
                                                              the quill…
I hear the Sphynx laughing on the inside
The sound of my quill running over the paper…
A huge hand crosses through me not being able to see it,
It sweeps everything up to the corner of the ceiling that is behind me,
And on the paper where I write, between it and the quill that writes
Lies the corpse of King Cheops, gazing up at me with wide open eyes,
And between our intersecting eyes runs the Nile
And the joyful flags of ornamented boats wandering
On a diffuse diagonal
Between me and what I think…

King Cheops' funerals in antique gold and Me!

IV

What tambourines the silence of this room!…
The walls are in Andalusia…
There are sensual dances in the fixed brightness of the light…

Suddenly the whole space stops...,
Stops, slips, unwraps...,
And in a corner of the ceiling, much further away than it is,
White hands open secret windows
To bouquets of falling violets
Outside it was a spring night
Me having my eyes shut...

V

Outside there is a whirlwind of sun, the carrousel horses...
Trees, stones, hills, are still inside me dancing...
Absolute night at the illuminated fair, moonlight on a sunny day outside,
And all the lights of the fair make noise from the walls of the backyard...
Ranches of girls with jugs on their heads
That pass outside, tired of being in the sun,
Mix with large sticky groups of people who walk through the fair,
People all mixed up with the stall lights, with the night and the moonlight,
And the two groups meet and penetrate each other
Until they form only one that is the two of them...
The fair and the lights of the fair and the people who walk in the fair,
And the night picks up the fair and raises it in the air,
They walk over the treetops full of sunlight,
They walk visibly under the rocks that shine in the sun,
They appear on the other side of the jugs that the girls carry on their heads,
And this whole spring landscape is the moon over the fair,
And the whole fair with noises and lights is the ground of this sunny day...

Suddenly someone shakes this double hour as if with a sieve
And mixed together, the dust of the two realities falls
Over my hands full of drawings of harbours
With great ships that set out without thinking of returning...
White and black gold dust over my fingers...
My hands are the steps of that girl that abandons the fair,
Alone and happy as the day it is today...

VI

The conductor shakes his baton,
The music breaks languid and sad...

Reminding me of my childhood, that day
When I threw a handball against a backyard wall
That had on one side
A sliding green dog, and on the other side
A blue horse running with a yellow jockey...

The music continues, and here it is in my childhood
At once between me and the conductor and the white wall,
The ball comes and goes, now a green dog,
Now a blue horse with a yellow jockey…

The whole theater is my backyard, my childhood
Is in every place, and the ball arrives playing music
A sad and vague music that strolls through my backyard
Dressed as a green dog becoming a yellow jockey.
(The ball spins quickly between me and the musicians…)

I throw it against my childhood and it
Crosses the whole theater at my feet
Playing with a yellow jockey and a green dog
And a blue horse that appears over the wall
Of my backyard… And the music shoots balls
At my childhood… And the backyard wall is made of gestures
From a baton and confused rotations of green dogs
And blue horses and yellow jockeys…

The whole theater is a white wall of music
Where a green dog runs after my longing
For my childhood, blue horse with a yellow jockey…

And from side to side, from right to left,
Where there are trees and between the branches close to the treetop
With orchestras playing music,
Where there are rows of balls in the store where I bought it
And the store clerk smiles amidst my childhood memories…

And the music stops like a falling wall,
The ball rolls down the cliff of my interrupted dreams,
And from the top of a blue horse, the conductor, yellow jockey becoming black,

Gives thanks, placing the baton on top of the fallen wall,
And he bends, smiling, with a white ball on his head,
White ball that disappears down his back…

March 8, 1914.

Fernando Pessôa.

ORPHEU
CONTRIBUTORS

ALFREDO PEDRO GUISADO (1891-1975) was a poet of Galician origin who contributed classically composed poems to *Orpheu*. He was also a journalist who opposed Salazar's dictatorship. He owned the "Irmãos Unidos" café in Rossio, where the oil portrait of Fernando Pessoa by Almada-Negreiros was exhibited.

ÁLVARO DE CAMPOS was a futurist and sensationist heteronym of Fernando Pessoa. According to Pessoa, he was born in Tavira in 1890. In "Portugal futurista" (1917), he published his "Ultimatum", one of the main texts of Portuguese futurism.

ÂNGELO DE LIMA (1872-1921) was diagnosed as insane and hospitalized in an asylum in 1901, until his death. He published poems in magazines, collected only after his death.

ANTÓNIO FERRO (1895-1956) was not a direct collaborator of *Orpheu,* but was asked by Sá-Carneiro, his friend, to be the editor of the journal, since the former was a minor at the time, and could not be charged if the magazine was prosecuted for transgressing moral norms.

CÔRTES RODRIGUES (1891-1971) was born in the Azores. His poems are linked to "Paulismo", a movement that originated in Symbolism. It is to him that Pessoa wrote his "Letter on the genesis of the heteronyms", fundamental to an understanding their origin.

EDUARDO GUIMARÃES (1892-1928), a friend of Ronald de Carvalho and Luís de Montalvor, was one of the main representatives of symbolist poetry in Brazil.

FERNANDO PESSOA (1888-1935), considered to be one of the greatest poets in the history of Portuguese literature, was misunderstood in his time, having published but a single book shortly before his death. The poem "Maritime Ode", written under the name Álvaro de Campos, is one of the main texts of *Orpheu*.

JOSÉ DE ALMADA-NEGREIROS (1893-1970), known mainly for his paintings and drawings, was also a poet and fiction writer. He called himself a Futurist from 1917 until his death, and was one of the main collaborators of the magazine "Portugal Futurista", where he published his manifesto "Futuristic ultimatum to the Portuguese generations of the 20th century".

JOSÉ PACHECO (1885-1934), an architect and graphic designer, who signed his name Pacheko in his futuristic phase, was one of the great supporters of modernism, contributing with his innovations to the originality of that aesthetic movement's publications.

LUÍS DE MONTALVOR (1892-1947) was a poet influenced by symbolism and a bridge between the poets of Portugal and Brazil, where he lived for some time. He was the first editor of Pessoa's poetry. He left behind little work of his own and died in tragic circumstances with his wife and daughter, when his car plunged into the river Tagus.

MÁRIO DE SÁ-CARNEIRO (1890-1916) had already published fiction and poetry when he encouraged Pessoa to join the publication of *Orpheu*. Financed by his father, *Orpheu* ended when his father withdrew his financial support. He lived the last years of his life in Paris where he committed suicide.

RAUL LEAL (1886-1964), philosopher and advocate of doctrines invented by himself such as paracletianism, was the author of the pamphlet "Sodom divinized" (1923), in which he advocated homosexuality. Leal's position was defended by Fernando Pessoa from the violent attacks of conservatives.

RONALD DE CARVALHO (1893-1935) was born in Rio de Janeiro. He was a traditionalist poet despite being one of *Orpheu's* original founders. He participated in Brazilian modernism until his death in a car accident.

SANTA-RITA PINTOR (1889-1918) was an eccentric figure who sought provocation and originality. He saw himself as a Futurist and was a friend of Sá-Carneiro in Paris. His family carried out the request in his will to destroy his work. Only a small portion was preserved.

VIOLANTE DE CYSNEIROS is the author of the poems written by Armando Cortes-Rodrigues, at Pessoa's request for there to be a female collaborator in *Orpheu*.

DAVID SWARTZ

Born in Canada, David Swartz has resided in Portugal since 2014 where he teaches English at NOVA University Lisbon. His translation of Nuno Júdice's *The Religious Mantle* was published by New Meridian Arts in 2019.

MÓNICA SOFIA GOMES GANHÃO

Born in Macau, Mónica Ganhão has lived most of her life in Lisbon where she is currently developing a PhD thesis on nineteenth-century Portuguese female novelists at the Faculty of Letters of the University of Lisbon.

NUNO JÚDICE

Nuno Júdice is a renowned essayist, poet, writer, novelist and professor from Portugal. His books include *Poesia Futurista Portuguese* (Faro 1916-1917) published in 1981 by Regra do Jogo and *A Era do Orpheu* (*The Orpheu Era*) published in 1986 by Editorial Teorema.

www.ingramcontent.com/pod-product-compliance
Lightning Source LLC
Chambersburg PA
CBHW051257250626
47155CB00009B/3329